revise

GCSE
French

Caroline Woods

with Tony Buzan

Hodder & Stoughton

A MEMBER OF THE HODDER HEADLINE GROUP

Acknowledgments

The author and publishers would like to thank the following for the use of material in this publication:

EDEXCEL (formerly ULEAC University of London Examinations & Assessment Council) *London Examinations* – *Modern Foreign Languages: French* in Chapter 1 Higher Task 1 (page 16); *L' Indépendant* no. 192 (page 2) August 10, 1996 in Chapter 6 Higher Task 3 (page 58); *Okapi* **Presse Bayard** no. 569 (page 4) 'Portez-vous des vêtements de marque?' September 23, 1995 in Chapter 7 Higher Task 1 (page 68), no. 581 March 23, 1996 'Ça c'est du sport' in Chapter 11 Reading Higher Exercise 2 (page 135), no. 583 April 27, 1995 'Ç'est ma planète' in Chapter 11 Reading Higher Exercise 3 (page 136); *Phosphore* **Presse Bayard** November, 1995 (pages 52 and 54) in Chapter 11 Listening Higher Exercise 3 (page 129), July–August 1996 (page 19) in Chapter 11 Reading Higher Exercise 4 (page 137); *Mikado* **Milan Presse** August 22–28, 1996 'Les clés de l'actualité junior' in Chapter 11 Listening Higher Exercise 1 (page 128), no. 150 April, 1996 (page 20) in Chapter 11 Reading Foundation/Higher Exercise 3 (page 135).

Every attempt has been made to obtain the required permission.

ISBN 0 340 66393 6

First published 1997
Impression number   10 9 8 7 6 5 4 3 2 1
Year   2002 2001 2000 1999 1998 1997

Designed and produced by Gecko Ltd, Bicester, Oxon
Printed in Great Britain for Hodder & Stoughton Educational, a division of Hodder Headline Plc, 338 Euston Road, London NW1 3BH by Scotprint Ltd, Musselburgh, Scotland.

Mind Maps: Christine Richsteiner
Illustrations: Kath Baxendale, Karen Donnelly,
   Andrea Norton, John Plumb, Dave Poole, Katherine Walker
Cover design: Amanda Hawkes
Cover illustration: Paul Bateman

Contents

Revision made easy

The four pages that follow contain a gold mine of information on how you can achieve success both at school and in your exams. Read them and apply the information, and you will be able to spend less, but more efficient, time studying, with better results. If you already have another *Hodder & Stoughton Revision Guide*, skim-read these pages to remind yourself about the exciting new techniques the books use, then move ahead to page 5.

This section gives you vital information on how to remember more *while* you are learning and how to remember more *after* you have finished studying. It explains

> **how to use special techniques to improve your memory**

> **how to use a revolutionary note-taking technique called Mind Maps that will double your memory and help you to write essays, use the language and answer exam questions**

> **how to read everything faster while at the same time improving your comprehension and concentration**

All this information is packed into the next four pages, so make sure you read them!

Your *amazing* memory

There are five important things you must know about your brain and memory to revolutionise your school life.

> **1** **how your memory ('recall') works *while* you are learning**

> **2** **how your memory works *after* you have finished learning**

> **3** **how to use Mind Maps – a special technique for helping you with all aspects of your studies**

> **4** **how to increase your reading speed**

> **5** **how to zap your revision**

1 Recall during learning – the need for breaks

When you are studying, your memory can concentrate, understand and remember well for between 20 and 45 minutes at a time. Then it *needs* a break. If you carry on for longer than this without one, your memory starts to break down! If you study for hours non-stop, you will remember only a fraction of what you have been trying to learn, and you will have wasted valuable revision time.

So, ideally, *study for less than an hour*, then take a five- to ten-minute break. During the break listen to music, go for a walk, do some exercise, or just daydream. (Daydreaming is a necessary brain-power booster – geniuses do it regularly.) During the break your brain will be sorting out what it has been learning, and you will go back to your books with the new information safely stored and organised in your memory banks. We recommend breaks at regular intervals as you work through the *Revision Guides*. Make sure you take them!

2 Recall after learning – the waves of your memory

What do you think begins to happen to your memory straight *after* you have finished learning something? Does it immediately start forgetting? No! Your brain actually *increases* its power and carries on remembering. For a short time after your study session, your brain integrates the information, making a more complete picture of everything it has just learnt. Only then does the rapid decline in memory begin, and as much as 80 per cent of what you have learnt can be forgotten in a day.

However, if you catch the top of the wave of your memory, and briefly review (look back over) what you have been revising at the correct time, the memory is stamped in far more strongly, and stays at the crest of the wave for a much longer time. To maximise your brain's power to remember, take a few minutes and use a Mind Map to review what you have learnt at the end of a day. Then review it at the end of a week, again at the end of a month, and finally a week before the exams. That way you'll ride your memory wave all the way to your exam – and beyond!

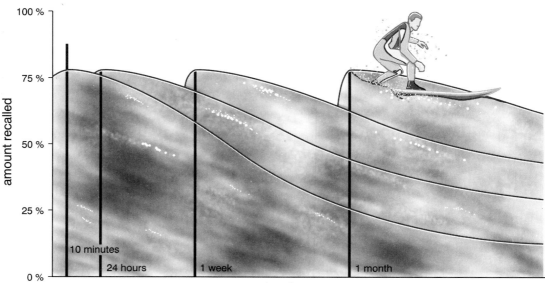

The graph shows amount recalled (y-axis, 0% to 100%) against review time (x-axis) with markers at 10 minutes, 24 hours, 1 week, and 1 month.

Amazing as your memory is (think of everything you actually do have stored in your brain at this moment) the principles on which it operates are very simple: your brain will remember if it (a) has an image (a picture or a symbol); (b) has that image fixed and (c) can link that image to something else.

3 The Mind Map® – a picture of the way you think

Do you *like* taking notes and making vocabulary lists? More importantly, do you like having to go back over and learn them before exams? Most students I know certainly do not! And how do you take your notes and make your lists? Most people take notes and make lists on lined paper, using blue or black ink. The result, visually, is *boring*! And what does your brain do when it is bored? It turns off, tunes out, and goes to sleep! Add a dash of colour, rhythm, imagination, and the whole process becomes much more fun, uses more of your brain's abilities, *and* improves your recall and understanding.

A Mind Map mirrors the way your brain works. It can be used for note-taking and gathering vocabulary phrases and language structures from books or in class, for reviewing what you have just studied, for revising, and for essay planning for coursework and in exams.

It uses all your memory's natural techniques to build up your rapidly growing 'memory muscle'.

You will find Mind Maps throughout this book. Study them, add some colour, personalise them, and then have a go at drawing your own – you'll remember them far better! Put them on your walls and in your files for a quick-and-easy review of the topic.

How to draw a Mind Map

● Start in the middle of the page with the page turned sideways. This gives your brain the maximum room for its thoughts.

● Always start by drawing a small picture or symbol. Why? Because a picture is worth a thousand words to your brain. And try to use at least three colours, as colour helps your memory even more.

● Let your thoughts flow, and write or draw your ideas on coloured branching lines connected to your central image. These key symbols and words are the headings for your topic. The Mind Map at the top of the next page shows you how to start.

● Then add facts, further items and ideas, time markers and tenses by drawing more, smaller, branches on to the appropriate main branches, just like a tree.

● Always print your word clearly on its line. Use only one word per line. The Mind Map at the foot of the next page shows you how to do this.

● To link ideas and thoughts on different branches, use arrows, colours, underlining, and boxes.

How to read a Mind Map

● Begin in the centre, the focus of your topic.

● The words/images attached to the centre are like chapter headings: read them next.

● Always read out from the centre, in every direction (even on the left-hand side, where you will have to read from right to left, instead of the usual left to right).

Using Mind Maps

Mind Maps are a versatile tool – use them for taking notes in class or from books, for solving problems, for brainstorming with friends, and for reviewing and revising for exams – their uses are endless! You will find them invaluable for planning essays for coursework and exams. Number your main branches in the order in which you want to use them and off you go – the main headings for your essay are done and all your ideas are logically organised!

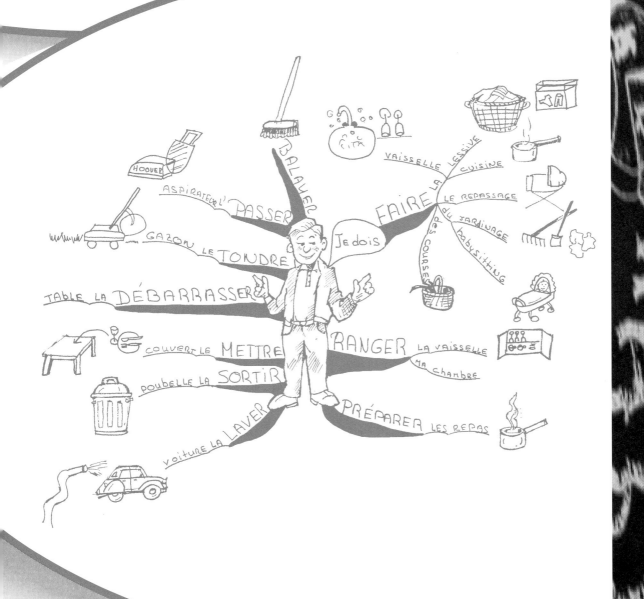

4 Super speed reading

It seems incredible, but it's been proved – the faster you read, the more you understand and remember! So here are some tips to help you to practise reading faster – you'll cover the ground more quickly, remember more, *and* have more time for revision!

★ Read the whole text (whether it's a lengthy book, a long passage or an exam paper) very quickly first, to give your brain an overall idea of what's ahead and get it working. (It's like sending out a scout to look at the territory you have to cover – it's much easier when you know what to expect!) Then read the text again for more detailed information.

★ Have the text a reasonable distance away from your eyes. In this way your eye/brain system will be able to see more at a glance, and will naturally begin to read faster.

★ Take in groups of words at a time. Rather than reading 'slowly and carefully' read faster, more enthusiastically. Your comprehension will rocket!

★ Take in phrases rather than single words while you read.

★ Use a guide. Your eyes are designed to follow movement, so a thin pencil underneath the lines you are reading, moved smoothly along, will 'pull' your eyes to faster speeds.

5 Helpful hints for exam revision

Start to revise at the beginning of the course. Cram at the start, not the end and avoid 'exam panic'!

Use Mind Maps throughout your course, and build a Master Mind Map for each subject – a giant Mind Map that summarises everything you know about the subject.

Use memory techniques such as mnemonics (verses or systems for remembering things like dates and events, or lists).

Get together with one or two friends to revise, compare Mind Maps, and discuss topics.

And finally...

● *Have fun while you learn* – studies show that those people who enjoy what they are doing understand and remember it more, and generally do it better.

● *Use your teachers* as resource centres. Ask them for help with specific topics and with more general advice on how you can improve your all-round performance.

● *Personalise your Revision Guide* by underlining and highlighting, by adding notes and pictures. Allow your brain to have a conversation with it!

Your brain is an amazing piece of equipment – learn to use it, and you, like thousands of students before you will be able to master French with ease. The more you understand and use your brain, the more it will repay you!

Tackling the tiers without tears

How do I use this book?

This French Revision Guide covers ten topics. Each topic is divided into two tier sections: Foundation and Higher. A numbered checklist at the beginning of each section lists the things you should know for each tier within that topic. Use the checklist by shading in the Fine or Help! buttons as you work through your revision to keep a record of your progress and to identify where you need to concentrate your efforts. You will also see how your memory and skills are growing.

The chapters contain all the vocabulary and structures that you need to achieve good GCSE grades for any of the exam boards. The language is presented in a way that is easy to follow and remember.

Find out from the start which tiers you have been entered for so that you can see which sections of the revision guide will be most useful to you. For example, if you were entered for all the Higher papers except in Writing, you would work through all the Foundation and Higher chapters but you could leave out the Higher tasks marked with the Writing symbol. In this way, you will be able to make the most of your revision time.

Use the checklist and the Notes / Options

Work through each chapter at your own pace: shade in the checklist (Fine/Help). For all of the items that you have shaded or ticked on the Help! button go on to read the Notes/Options on that point.

Then move on to the Test Yourself tasks which include exercises within the four skills (Listening, Speaking, Reading, Writing); these will help you to recall the content of the chapter and to give you some exam practice. Remember always to mark your answers using the upside-down key. If your answer is not satisfactory, look back at the Notes/Options on the points that have troubled you.

Before moving on from one chapter to the next, you should look back at the checklist to be certain that you are confident with all of the items on the list. You should have shaded all of the Fine buttons before you move on.

Make the most of the Mind Maps

Each of the ten topics is linked to the Mind Maps in the coloured section; these connect the ideas and vocabulary in the chapters to help you learn the vital vocabulary. Watch out for the signpost showing you the way to interesting Mind Maps.

There is a summary Mind Map on page 93.

Have a go at making your own Mind Maps. Use symbols and pictures on them, it will really help you to retain the vocabulary and ideas. There are also grammar Mind Maps to help you to revise the crucial tenses.

A practice mock exam

Finally, there is a mock exam in Chapter 11. It is a full mock exam for Listening, Speaking, Reading and Writing. Work through the tier which you intend to tackle in the exam for each exam part.

A grammar reference

You will find the grammar explanations in Chapter 12 very useful as your revision progresses.

Please write on me! Make notes as you go, use higlighter pens, and make your own Mind Maps. This is one book on which you can make your 'mark'! Feel free to make notes to yourself in the book. Keep blank paper and coloured pens by you as you revise in case you feel an urge to Mind Map! Revising should be an 'active' use of time so that you remember more effectively!

Train your memory

Your memory improves the more you use it – according to scientific research! Read through pages 1–4 again. Realise that you cannot leave all of that French revision until the night before your exam – there just won't be enough time!

Plan out the time before your French exam so that you revise a little every day allowing your mind to absorb the information. Give more time to the topics that you find most difficult. Bear in mind the other subjects you are taking and juggle your revision time carefully.

Some people find that they are most receptive to learning and memorising in the mornings, but only you can decide what works best for you. Be aware of what are the hardest topics and structures for you, and don't leave them to the last minute!

TEN TOP TIPS for learning vocabulary

1 Use different coloured pens to highlight masculine and feminine words on Mind Maps.

2 Draw an item or symbol for key vocabulary.

3 Don't try to learn more than ten words at a time.

4 Take ten minutes to make a Mind Map. Then, after a break, take another ten minutes to write out the vocabulary using the Mind Map.

5 Use a list of ten words, start at the bottom and work upwards, as well as downwards.

6 Visualise each item of vocabulary as you say the word in French.

7 Record yourself – play it back and imagine the item again.

8 Ask friends, brothers, sisters or parents to test you on vocabulary.

9 Remember that with regular effort you can build a bigger vocabulary and recall it.

10 Think positive. Vocabulary is the key and the more often you learn small chunks, the easier it gets.

Are you sitting comfortably?

You need to be at ease when you are revising. Here are some tips to help you choose an ideal working environment.

LOCATION Never revise in the kitchen or the living room with the TV on or with brothers or sisters around. Find a place that is quiet and where there are no distractions. If you find it hard to revise at home, you could go to your library.

LIGHTING Natural light is best. If you can, sit by a window. If you have to work in artificial light, try to use a lamp rather than fluorescent lighting as this can give you eye strain. Avoid shadows; make sure that the light comes from your left if you are right-handed, and from your right if you are left-handed.

HEATING If you are too warm while you are revising, you might find that you start falling asleep – not ideal for training your memory! Fresh air helps concentration so open the windows while you are working, or at least during your short breaks.

SPACE Organise your desk or table so that your books, notes, dictionaries, pens and paper are within easy reach. If you have to keep getting up to look for things you will be easily distracted.

POSITION Make sure your chair is at the right height and keeping your back straight while you are revising. You might get back-ache if you sit awkwardly. Never work in an armchair or lying on your bed: you will be too relaxed to take much in!

FUEL Meals are very important. Pay as much attention to your food intake as does an athlete training for a competition! Limit the amount of sugary and fatty things you eat as these increase irritability and can disrupt concentration. Likewise, stimulating drinks (such as coffee and tea) can revive you in the short term, but they might also disturb your sleep pattern and affect your memory if you're tired.

Which exams will I be taking?

For your GCSE French exam, if you are following a MEG, NEAB, EDEXCEL (formerly ULEAC) or WJEC course, you will be assessed on four areas of language skills: Listening, Speaking, Reading and Writing. You will either sit an exam for each of these skills or you will do a coursework option (see below).

Which tier: Foundation or Higher?

You can take the different exam parts at either the Foundation or Higher tier. This gives you the following three options:

- You take exams in all four language skills at the Foundation tier (possible grades G – C)

- You take exams in all four language skills at the Higher tier (possible grades D – A*)

- You 'mix and match'. This is a mixture of tiers for the different exam parts (Listening, Speaking, Reading, Writing), according to your strengths and weaknesses. This might limit your grades.

What grades can I get if I mix tiers?

A Foundation tier paper equals a possible total of up to 5 points – e.g. C = 5 points.

A Higher tier paper equals a possible total of up to 8 points (but you *must* score at least 3 points on a Higher tier paper or you will get zero points!)

If you do the coursework option, up to 8 points will be available depending on the difficulty of the task and on how well you do!

Your total number of points for the four different skills areas will be added together to give an overall points score out of 32. The points are then converted to a final grade.

G = 2 – 5 points

F = 6 – 9 points

E = 10 – 13 points

D = 14 – 17 points

C = 18 – 21 points

B = 22 – 25 points

A = 26 – 29 points

A* = 30 – 32 points

Listening Speaking Reading Writing

F   F   H   F

5   +   5   +   8   +   5

=   23   =   B grade!

So, if you were to do three Foundation tier papers (3 × 5 possible points) and one Higher tier paper (1 × 8 possible points = total 23 points) the highest grade you could possibly be awarded would a B.

> Remember! Make sure you know which tier you are doing for which paper before you start revising and before the exam, and check the tier on your exam paper on the day. You can only do one tier for each paper, so check that it is the correct one!

What is the coursework option?

- **Writing** Most exam boards offer the Writing coursework option which means that you can build up a file of written work during Years 10 and 11; usually, three pieces of work are submitted to the board.

  Find out from your teacher if you will be doing the coursework option. If you are, you will receive lots of guidance. You will be told which subjects to write about, how much you have to write (this will vary from 40 – 150 words usually depending on the type of task and the final grade you are aiming for). Your teacher will mark this work initially, so you will have a good idea of how well you are progressing.

  There are lots of writing tasks in this book, together with tips on how to impress the examiners. So, work through the chapters in the order of the topics you meet at school. This will help you to practise for your coursework tasks. One piece of work, at least, will have to be done in class in 'controlled conditions'. You will still be able to use dictionaries and reference materials, but you won't get any help from people in the classroom.

- **Speaking** EDEXCEL (formerly ULEAC) offers a Speaking coursework option. If you do this you will build up evidence of your performance on cassette during Years 10 and 11. You will be expected to perform both role play and conversation tasks. Ask your teacher for further details .

You cannot do both Writing and Speaking coursework options.

What happens with a SEG Modular course?
If you are following a SEG Modular course, you will be assessed both during the course in Years 10 and 11 and at the end of your course in Year 11.

The SEG syllabus requires you to work through four modules of work as follows:

Module 1 tests Listening, Speaking and Reading through coursework (February, Year 10) and concentrates on these topics: Personal Details, Family and Pets, Home and Local Environment, Local and Leisure Environment, Health and School.

Module 2 tests listening and Reading through an end of Module Test (June, Year 10) and concentrates on these topics: Tourist Information, Travel by Bus, Directions, Money and Banks, Shopping, Food and Drink, Entertainment, Emergencies.

Module 3 (February, Year 11) tests Speaking and Reading through coursework and concentrates on Holidays and Accommodation, Travel and Transport, Bank, Services, Weather, Directions, Shopping.

Module 4 tests Listening, Speaking, Reading and Writing through exam (Year 11, June) and concentrates on Personal Identity and Relationships, the Environment, School, Future Plans, Work, Spending Money and Health.

Remember! The topics covered in the modules feature in this book – work through them in the order you meet the topics in your modules 1 – 4.

During the exam
- Structure your time so that you have enough time to answer all of the questions. Don't spend too long on one question. First answer the questions you can do easily and then go back to the more difficult ones.
- Answer all the questions.
- Look carefully at the number of marks you can get for each question. For example three marks means you must give three items of information in your answer.
- Stick to the point. Give opinions and reasons wherever you can and use the different tenses where appropriate. Don't pad out your answer with irrelevant material, it will be obvious that you can't answer the question.

- Plan your answers, expecially for the writing paper. Draw a quick Mind Map.
- Write clearly. Ask for some blank sheets if you want to write out notes or plan with Mind Maps. Remember to cross out neatly any work that you don't want the examiner to mark.
- Leave some time at the end to look over your answers and for a final dictionary check.
- Remember to answer in the correct language (see page 9).

Using a dictionary in an exam
You can use a bilingual dictionary during Reading and Writing exams, and some boards (e.g. NEAB and WJEC) also allow you to use a dictionary before and after the cassette is played in the Listening exam. All boards allow you to use a dictionary while preparing your Speaking exam, but not during the actual exam. Here are some key points to remember:

TIME SAVING Using a dictionary takes (and can waste) valuable time in an exam. Use one only when it is absolutely necessary. Do not look up every single work you don't know on a long reading text – you may not need to know every word. But, do use a dictionary to check the meaning of words in questions if you are unsure.

SPEED Practise using a dictionary so that you can build up your 'search speed'. If possible use the same edition that you will be using in the exam. This will mean you waste less time and that you'll feel more confident about how to use one well. Make sure that you know what the abbreviations mean.

DON'T PANIC Learn as much vocabulary as you can before the exam but remember you will probably not know every word in the exam – so don't panic!

LAST RESORT Work through as much of each exercise as you can without using a dictionary. It is there to help you in an emergency.

Understanding instructions
Learn the phrases on page 9. You will then know exactly the way in which you should answer the questions (e.g. tick the box). If you do not understand the instructions you will not do yourself justice.

Most of the instructions on your exam papers will be in French. Some exam boards use the 'vous' form, e.g. complétez, others use the 'tu' form, e.g. complète. Make sure you know the following:

Arrange / Arrangez … les mots dans le bon ordre	Arrange … the words in the right order
Choisis / Choisissez … les bonnes phrases, la bonne lettre	Choose … the right sentences, the right letter
Coche / Cochez … la case appropriée, la bonne case	Tick … the right box
Complète / Complétez … les détails, la grille	Complete … the details, the grid
Copie / Copiez …	Copy …
Corrige / Corrigez … les détails, les fautes, les erreurs	Correct … the details, the mistakes
Décris / Décrivez …	Describe …
Demande / Demandez … pourquoi	Ask … why
Dessine / Dessinez … une flèche	Draw … an arrow
Dis / Dites …	Say …..
Donne / Donnez les détails	Give the details
En chiffres	In figures
Ecris / Ecrivez … le mot qui ne va pas avec les autres	Write … the word which doesn't go with the others
… les numéros, les lettres	… the numbers, the letters
… qui correspondent … une carte, une lettre, en français	… which match … a card, a letter, in French
Encercle / Encerclez oui ou non	Circle (draw a circle) round yes or no
Explique / Expliquez … pourquoi, comment	Explain … why, how
Fais / Faites une liste	Make a list
Finis / Finissez	Finish
Imagine / Imaginez	Imagine
Indique / Indiquez	Indicate

Lis / Lisez … le texte, l'article	Read … the text, the article
Met / Mettez … les dessins dans le bon ordre	Put the drawings … in the right order
Note / Notez … les détails qui manquent	Note down … the missing details
Où est / sont …?	Where is / are … ?
Ou	Or
Pose / Posez des questions	Ask questions
Prépare / Préparez … un dépliant	Prepare … a leaflet
Quand?	When?
Que veut dire …?	What does … mean?
Quel problème?	Which problem?
Quelle erreur?	Which mistake?
Qui …?	Who …?
Regarde / Regardez l'image	Look at the picture
Remercie / Remerciez …	Thank …
Remplis / Remplissez … la grille, le formulaire	Fill in … the grid, the form
Réponds / Répondez aux questions en français	Answer the questions in French
Tourne / Tournez la page	Turn the page
Trouve / Trouvez … l'erreur, la bonne réponse	Find … the mistake, the correct answer
Utilise / Utilisez les symboles	Use the symbols
Vous n'aurez pas besoin de toutes les lettres	You will not need all the letters
Vrai ou faux?	True or false?

Last minute tips!

If you write in the wrong language you will not get any marks. For Reading and Listening exams, up to one-fifth of the marks may be awarded to questions which have English instructions or require answers written in English. Remember, if the instructions are English you have to write out an answer in English. If the instructions are in French you have to write out an answer in French.

Listening

- If you can use a dictionary before the exam (NEAB, WJEC) read through the questions quickly, and look up ones you're not sure about. Use the time at the end to check for words you need to write in the answers.

- Remember that you don't need to write in full sentences.

- Look carefully at the pictures in the questions.

- If you miss a question, don't panic, keep listening, you can have another 'go' in the second listen through!

- Write in the correct language!

- Don't agonise over a spelling; provided your *message is clear* examiners will tolerate mistakes!

Speaking

- Don't panic! Your teacher is there to help and is probably as nervous as you are about performing well!

- Remember your cue card if you are doing a presentation and arrive five minutes early.

- Use the preparation time well, use a dictionary to look up items shown in visual cues or the role plays.

- Read the English settings – they are there to explain the situation, put you at ease and to help!

- Try to spot the 'unexpected element' in the second Foundation, or the first Higher role play.

- While preparing, think what the examiner's lead-in question might be if you have a cue which says Répondez à la question, and how you could answer.

- If you don't understand a question or want something repeated, say so – Je n'ai pas compris la question. Répétez s'il vous plaît. This will give you a few seconds and keeps the French flowing!

- Remember: to get a C grade you need to use past, present and future tenses. Learn a few phrases in each of these tenses very thoroughly on each topic.

- Smile as you go in, it will relax you!

- Remember to work out exactly where you went on holiday last year, what you did last weekend, last night, this morning (perfect tense) and what you will do tonight, this weekend, in the summer, next year (future tense). Try not to fish around for ideas in the exam room – have your ideas 'straight' before you go in so that you only have to recall the appropriate phrases in French.

Reading

- Do not use a dictionary to look up every word you do not know.

- Read through the text and questions once before you even attempt to answer any questions or use the dictionary.

- Check that you understand the instructions.

- Examiners are checking that you have understood. Examiners will not deduct marks for incorrect spellings. But your message should be clear to gain marks.

- Try not to leave gaps – make an intelligent guess rather than leave a gap! You do not have to write in full sentences but, again, the message should be clear.

Writing

- Read the question at least twice before you start.

- Check the instructions.

- Use a dictionary to check the meanings of words in the question if you are at all unsure.

- Plan your answer using a Mind Map so that you cover all the communication points.

- On longer answers, examiners will look for accurate French, so check spellings and tenses very carefully.

- Do not use the dictionary to 'experiment with new phrases' – stick to what you know and can say well.

> If your exam is tomorrow, take a break and have a long bath! You could flick through the Mind Map section of this book for 20 minutes and then have a rest. Let your mind relax before the big day!

Bon courage!

Caroline Woods

1

It's all about yourself!

Match up the checklist items with the Notes/Options below. Concentrate on the questions that you are less confident about and where you need some help. The signposts will tell you when there is a Mind Map to help you learn the vocabulary in a certain area. These are on pages 94 – 96.

Help is at hand!

Notes/Options

1 Comment tu t'appelles?
Je m'appelle …

2 Tu es de quelle nationalité?
Je suis anglais(e).

ecossais(e), irlandais(e), gallois(e)
– *For girls add an 'e'!*

3 Tu as quel âge?
J'ai 16 ans.

16 = seize not six!

Quelle est la date de ton anniversaire?

Make sure you know the months.

C'est le 12 février.

4 Décris-toi s'il te plaît.

assez = quite

Je suis assez grand(e) et de taille moyenne.

petite = small
de taille moyenne = of medium build

J'ai les cheveux blonds et courts.

courts = short

Je suis timide, sympa et modeste!

timide = shy
sympa = nice

5 Tu as des frères ou des soeurs?
Non je suis enfant unique.

= I'm an only child.

Oui j'ai une soeur et un frère.
    demi-frère
    demi-soeur

= step-brother
= step-sister

Moi

checklist
What you need to know

How do you feel about these? In French, can you:

		Fine	Help!
1	say and spell your name?	✓	
2	give your nationality?	✓	
3	give your age and birthday?	✓	
4	describe yourself (physical appearance and character)?	✓	
5	give the same details about your family?	✓	
6	talk about your pets (size and colour)?	✓	
7	say where you live and spell it out?	✓	
8	say how you feel (ill, well, tired, hungry, thirsty, hot, cold, better)?	✓	
9	say where you have a pain?	✓	
10	ask for items at a chemist's?	✓	
11	call for help?	✓	

Ma soeur s'appelle Catherine. Elle est amusante*, mince et intelligente*.

*– Adjectives marked * end in 'e' to describe a girl.*

Mon frère s'appelle Paul. Il est amusant, et assez grand mais il est egoïste.

egoïste = selfish

Paul a 12 ans, Catherine a 14 ans.

Not Paul ~~est~~ 12 ans!

Décris ton père / ta mère? Ma mère s'appelle Anne. Elle est gentille. Elle a 40 ans.

gentille = nice

Mon père s'appelle Mike. Il est calme. Il a 42 ans.

calme = easy going

There's a great Mind Map to help you find your way round your family on page 94. Remember to revise numbers 1 – 100, and make sure you know all the ages of your family! Fill in the blank boxes on the Mind Map with the ages of members of your family.

6 Tu as un animal domestique?
Non je n'ai pas d'animal.
Je n'ai pas de / d'

= I haven't got

Oui j'ai un chat / chien, etc.
Il s'appelle Snowy –
il est blanc et il a deux ans.

Another Mind Map on page 94 has been designed to help you revise animals.

7 Où habites-tu?
J'habite 24 Baker Road.

Ça s'écrit comment?
Ça s'écrit B-A-K-E-R   R-O-A-D.

= How do you write it?

Listen to the alphabet on the cassette (Side 1, Chapter 1). Then check that you can spell out your name and address. You could also practise spelling the names of the people in your family.

You'll soon need to make sure you know the colours. Check the Mind Map on page 94.

How's your memory?

AGE + EYES + HAIR	
J'ai	16 ans
Il a / Elle a	les yeux bleus les cheveux longs

SIZE + PERSONALITY	
Je suis	grand(e) / petit(e)*
Il est	intelligent
Elle est	amusante
* For girls add an 'e'!	

Going for a C?

Expand your descriptions with basic opinions and give simple reasons for your views. You could use, for example:

J'aime ♥   Je n'aime pas ✗

J'adore ♥♥   Je déteste ✗✗

You could also learn and use describing details such as **sympa** or **méchant** so that you can say why you like or dislike something or someone.

8 Comment vas-tu?

= How are you?

Je suis malade / fatigué(e).
Ça ne va pas du tout.
J'ai faim / soif.
J'ai chaud / froid.

= I'm ill / tired.
= I'm not at all well.
= I'm hungry / thirsty.
= I'm hot / cold.

9 Où as-tu mal?

= Where does it hurt?

J'ai mal à …

+ *part of body.*

Take a look at the Mind Map on page 95 to help you feel more confident about saying which parts of the body are sore or feeling ill. Try to relate the vocabulary to your own body so that you know what you're talking about!

10 A la pharmacie = At the chemist's

The Mind Maps on page 96 will help you to memorise the important vocabulary here. Don't forget to picture what you're asking for: for example a <u>tube</u> of toothpaste and a <u>bottle</u> of aspirins.

11 If you've got this far you shouldn't feel like this!

AU SECOURS!

HODDER REVISION GUIDE

TAKE A BREAK!

Now try the Test yourself exercises! When you've done them, look back at the Checklist on page 11 – you should now feel fine about all the questions.

Test yourself

Task 1

Record the checklist questions and play back the cassette stopping after each question to give the answer. See how long you can talk about your family without being interrupted. Can you manage a minute? Well done! Practise the questions and answers with a friend.

Task 2

Ecrivez une lettre (60–80 mots) à un(e) correspondant(e) sur votre famille.

Task 3

Listen to the cassette (Side 1, Chapter 1) and have a go at this exercise.
Remplissez les détails en français. Ecoutez deux fois.

Christophe

Age?.....seize.....¹ ans

Date d'anniversaire?.....22 septembre.....²

Mère-âge?.....43.....³ ans

Père-âge?.....41.....⁴ ans

Soeurs/frères? combien?.....1½ un soeur.....⁵

Animal?.....lapin.....⁶ + ...chat.....⁷

Nom du village .....Lurviel × Murviel.....⁸

Check your answers. More than five? Well done!

Task 4

Have a quick look at the Checklist again, then write out as much as you can without looking things up. When you've finished ask a friend to read it – pick someone who is also learning French. Can they understand it? Give yourself a point for each bit of information they can understand (for example: J'ai un frère = one point). More than six? Excellent!

Do you remember these?

Start off	Cher + boy's name
	Chère + girl's name
Finish off	A bientôt
	Amitiés
	Amicalement

TASK 3
1 16; **2** 22 septembre; **3** 43; **4** 41; **5** une soeur; **6** un lapin; **7** un chat; **8** MURVIEL.

Answers

Moi

checklist
What you need to know

How do you feel about these? In French, can you:

	Fine	Help!
1 do the Foundation checklist on page 11?	✓	
2 describe your friends (how they look, character)?		
3 say how you feel about your family and friends?		
4 make arrangements to see a doctor / dentist?		
5 ask and answer questions about medical treatment?		
6 give details about your lifestyle (healthy / unhealthy)?		

It's all about yourself!

Match up the checklist items with the Notes/Options below. Concentrate on the questions that you are less confident about and where you need some help. The signposts will tell you when there is a Mind Map to help you learn the vocabulary in a certain area. These are on pages 94 – 96.

Help is at hand!

Notes/Options

1 *Look back again at the Foundation Checklist. If you feel confident, carry on!*

2 Décris ta meilleure copine. Elle s'appelle Chloë. Elle a 16 ans. Elle est grande et mince. Elle a les cheveux blonds et les yeux bleus. Elle est drôle et sympa.

drôle = amusante

Décris ton meilleur copain.

Il s'appelle Alex. Il a 15 ans. Il a les yeux marron et les cheveux courts et noirs. Quelquefois il est bête et il m'énerve mais d'habitude il me fait rire.

marron = brown
– *No 's' is added.*
courts = short
bête = stupid
= he annoys me

= he makes me laugh

3 Tu t'entends bien avec ton frère / père / copain?

= Do you get on well with …?

Tu t'entends bien avec ta soeur / mère / copine?

Oui je m'entends bien avec lui / avec elle.

avec lui = with him
avec elle = with her

Non je ne m'entends pas bien avec lui / elle.

= No I don't get on well with him / her.

The Mind Map on page 94 represents a large family. You could be creative and draw a similar map of your own family.

Reasons for liking	Reasons for disliking
je l'aime parce qu'…	je ne l'aime pas parce qu'…
il / elle est sympa	il / elle est bête
il / elle est amusant(e)	il / elle m'enerve
il / elle m'aide	il / elle est egoïste
il / elle me fait rire	il / elle prend mes affaires

4 Prendre un rendez-vous — = To make an appointment

Je peux voir le docteur / le dentiste? — = Can I see the doctor / dentist?

le docteur = } doctor
le médecin = }

C'est urgent.

Je voudrais un rendez-vous cet après-midi / demain matin. — = I'd like an appointment this afternoon / tomorrow morning.

Take a look at the medical instructions vocabulary on page 96, and learn the phrases – especially those that might be said to you when you're feeling unwell.

5 Qu'est-ce que je dois faire? — = What should I do?
Est-ce que je dois rester au lit? — = Should I stay in bed?

Je dois prendre des médicaments? — = Should I take some medicine?
Il faut une ordonnance? — = Do I need a prescription?

C'est grave? — = Is it serious?

Remember the Mind Map on page 96 that shows the answers to these questions and on page 95 for where you might feel the pain!

6 Tu as un régime équilibré? — = Do you have a balanced diet?

Oui je mange bien – je mange de façon équilibrée, par exemple de la viande, des légumes, des fruits et des produits laitiers. — = dairy products

Je ne saute pas les repas. Je ne mange pas trop de sucre. C'est bon / mauvais pour la santé. — = I don't skip meals. trop de = too much = It's healthy / unhealthy.

Il ne faut pas …
… fumer / boire de l'alcool / se droguer
… parce que ça nuit à la santé. — = You shouldn't . . . = . . . smoke / drink alcohol / take drugs = . . . because it damages your health.

Going for an A?

Be prepared to give details about your lifestyle such as what you eat / don't eat and which sports you practise (when and how often?). Be ready to give your opinion and give a reason.

Opinion 'starters'		
Je pense que		bête
Je crois que	+ c'est	dangereux
		bien

How's your memory?

pourquoi? = why?
parce que = because

Comment éviter le stress . . .

un peu de travail

un peu de révision

une bonne alimentation

un peu de repos   et un peu d'exercice

+ 8 heures de sommeil

Test yourself

Task 1

Listen to the cassette (Side 1, Chapter 1) and answer the questions in English.

La santé

At school, for Technology, you are doing a project on health and healthy eating. You decide to interview your penfriend's father to find out if people in France are aware of the importance of healthy eating.

Listen to what he says and take notes in English.

1 How did he know he was unfit? (two details)   2 marks

2 What made him do something about it?   1 mark

3 How did he alter his diet? (two details)   2 marks

4 What other action did he take?   1 mark

5 What criticism does he make of technological progress?   1 mark

6 What example does he give of the way motorcars have changed people's habits for the worse?   1 mark

Task 2

Here is some role play practice. You ring up to make an appointment at the doctor's. You feel tired and feverish and want to see him this evening.

1 Saluez l'employée et demandez un rendez-vous.

2 Expliquez vos symptômes.

3 Dites quand vous voulez voir le docteur.

4 Problème, il n'est pas libre ce soir! Que dites-vous?

5 Confirmez l'heure (10h 30) du rendez-vous.

Task 3

Ecrivez un article (100 mots) sur votre régime et votre santé. Etes-vous en forme?

(Before you tackle this writing exercise look back at the Checklist 6 and make sure you can answer the question as fully as possible.)

Remember to look back at the Checklist to see how much you've learned.
Well done – you've finished the chapter!

Chez moi

checklist
What you need to know

How do you feel about these questions? In French, can you:

	Fine	Help!
1 give your address?		
2 say whether you live in a house or a flat?		
3 describe your house / flat, and say where it is?		
4 name the rooms, and say how many there are?		
5 find out about the rooms in somebody else's house?		
6 describe your room (contents, colour, size) and say where it is?		
7 give a description of the rooms, and say what you do in each room?		
8 say if you have a garden and, if so, describe it?		
9 give information about or ask about having a bath or a shower?		
10 give information and find out about eating and other household routines?		
11 say what jobs you do around the house?		

Around the home

The Mind Maps on pages 97 – 99 will help you memorise the necessary vocabulary to talk about the rooms in your house along with their contents and the things you do in each room. Make full use of these maps as you work through this chapter. Remember that the more creative you are in your learning the more you'll know on the day of the exam. The more confident you are the better your results!

Help is at hand!

Notes/Options

1 Où habites-tu?
J'habite (à) Southport.
C'est une ville près de Liverpool.

un village = a village
près de = near

Où est Southport?
C'est dans le nord-ouest de l'Angleterre.

le sud = south
l'est = east
le nord = north
l'ouest = west

– Be prepared to spell the road name.

Quel est ton adresse?
C'est . . .

2 Tu habites une maison ou un appartement?
J'habite une maison.

3 Où se trouve ta maison?
C'est en ville.
dans la banlieue
à la campagne

= in the suburbs
= in the countryside

Comment est ta maison?

comment est . . .? = what is . . . like?

Ma maison est grande.
petite
assez
assez grande

= small
= quite
= quite big

C'est une maison mitoyenne

= semi detached

C'est une maison individuelle.

= detached

Look at the Mind Map on page 99.

Comment est ton appartement?
Mon appartement est grand
– c'est dans
un immeuble = block of flats
au deuxième étage. = on the second floor
au premier étage = on the first floor

4/5 Combien de pièces y a-t-il?
Il y a huit pièces – le salon, la salle à manger, le bureau, trois chambres et la salle de bains. Il y a aussi une cave.

il y a = there is / are
le bureau = the study

une cave = a cellar

6 Qu'est-ce qu'il y a dans ta chambre?
Il y a un lit, une commode, une armoire, une chaise, une table et une télévision.

Revise colours! Take another look at the Mind Map on page 94.

De quelle couleur est ta chambre?
Ma chambre est blanche, la moquette = the carpet
est bleue et
les rideaux = the curtains
sont bleus.

Où est ta chambre?
Elle est / C'est au premier étage, à côté de la salle de bains.

à côté de = next to
en face de = opposite

7 Comment sont les pièces chez toi?

= What are the rooms at your house like?

Use the Mind Map on page 98 to help you describe the different rooms in your house.

Que fais-tu dans ta chambre / la salle à manger?
Qu'est-ce qu'on fait dans le salon?
On regarde la télévision.
On écoute des CD.

Que fais-tu? = What do you do?
– *If you hear* on *in a question, such as* Qu'est-ce qu'on fait … ? *you will need to use* on *in the answer.*

There is another Mind Map on page 99 which is designed to help you say what you do in the different rooms of your house. After looking at the map, how many activities can you remember in French? Keep trying until you can say at least three for each place.

8 Est-ce qu'il y a un jardin chez toi?
Oui il y a un grand jardin.

Comment est ton jardin?

des arbres = some trees

Il y a des fleurs, des arbres et une pelouse.

des fleurs = some flowers
une pelouse = a lawn

If you've got a mental block about what you might do in the garden, take a look again at the Mind Map on page 98.

9 Est-ce que je peux . . . ? = Can I . . . ?

 … prendre un bain?

 … prendre une douche?

– *Remember to say please!* S'il te plaît *to a friend, but* s'il vous plaît *to an adult, such as a penfriend's parent.*

Où est la salle de bains?

= Where is the bathroom?

Je peux avoir une serviette s'il vous plaît?

= Please can I have a towel?

Je peux avoir du savon s'il vous plaît?

= Please can I have some soap?

 La douche ne marche pas!

= The shower isn't working!
le robinet = the tap

Revise telling the time (page 121) to be able to say at what time you do certain things.

10 A quelle heure est-ce que tu prends ton petit déjeuner?

Je prends le petit déjeuner à huit heures.

le petit déjeuner = breakfast
le déjeuner = lunch
le dîner = evening meal

A quelle heure est-ce que tu quittes la maison le matin?
Je quitte la maison à huit heures et demie.

le matin = in the morning

A quelle heure est-ce que tu te lèves?
Je me lève à sept heures.

= What time do you get up?

A quelle heure est-ce que tu te couches?
Je me couche à 10 heures et demie.

= What time do you go to bed?

11 Que fais-tu pour aider chez toi?
Je fais la vaisselle, je range ma chambre et je lave la voiture.

= What do you do to help at home?
= I do the washing up
je range = I tidy up

Going for a C?

Time markers	
d'habitude	= normally
quelquefois	= sometimes
souvent	= often
puis	= then
ensuite	= next
après	= afterwards
tous les jours	= every day
toujours	= always

Give as many details as possible, say *when*, *where* and *how often* things happen at home.

Give simple opinions such as **J'aime** / **Je n'aime pas**.

Use the perfect tense (see pages 122 and 141) to talk about what you did last night and the future tense (see pages 124 and 143) to talk about what you will do at home tonight / next weekend / tomorrow.

In the role play exercises, be prepared to listen to the teacher – you will have one task starting: **répondez à la question** . . .
As you prepare your role play, try to think ahead to what the question might be.

– *Use a selection of the time markers listed above.*

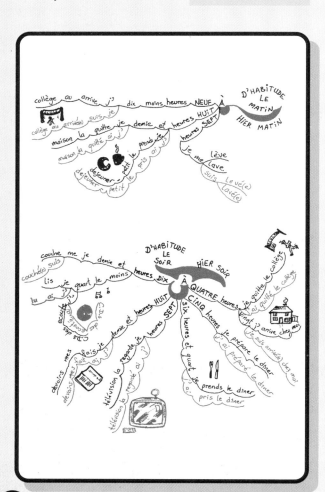

Test yourself

Task 1

Record the Checklist questions and then answer them all in French without looking at the notes. You might need a few attempts before getting them all right.

Now try to talk for a minute about your room (size, contents, colour) – whenever you get a bit stuck, just think of, or look at, the Mind Map on page 98 to help.

Task 2

Here's a role play exercise: you arrive at a French friend's house and you want to have a shower.

1 Posez la question …

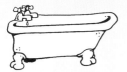 'où'

2 Dites ce que vous voulez.

3 Posez la question.

4 Dites ce que vous voulez.

Task 3

Write to a friend, using 60 – 80 words, about your home and daily routines. Refer back to the Notes/Options if you need some help. Remember to use **Cher** or **Chère** to start, and **Amitiés** or **Amicalement** to finish.

When you've written the letter, ask a friend who is also learning French to read it. Give yourself a point for each detail they understand.

More than eight points? Brilliant!

Task 4

Draw a Mind Map about what you did at home last night. Start by using **Hier soir** in the centre.

The following structures might be helpful:

j'ai mangé	= I ate
j'ai bu	= I drank
j'ai lu	= I read
j'ai pris	= I took
je suis allé(e)	= I went
je me suis couché(e)	= I went to bed
j'ai regardé	= I watched
j'ai aidé	= I helped
j'ai travaillé	= I worked
j'ai fait	= I did / made
je suis arrivé(e)	= I arrived
– Note: girls add the extra 'e'.	

Chez moi

checklist
What you need to know

How do you feel about these questions? In French, can you:

	Fine	Help!
1 answer the questions on the Foundation Checklist on page 18?		

If you've ticked the Help! box, go back to the Foundation Notes/Options and revise!

2 discuss and express opinions about meals, meal times and eating habits?		
3 talk about your daily routines in the past and future?		
4 say you'll help out, or ask for help around the house?		
5 say how you share jobs at home?	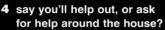	
6 say if you share a room?		

Around the home

The Mind Maps on pages 97 – 99 will help you memorise the necessary vocabulary to talk about the rooms in your house along with their contents and the things you do in each room. Make full use of these maps as you work through this chapter. Remember that the more creative you are in your learning the more you'll know on the day of the exam. The more confident you are the better your results!

Help is at hand!

Notes/Options

1 *Once you've looked back at the Foundation Checklist and feel confident, carry on!*

2 Quel est ton plat préféré?

Mon plat préféré est …

> = What's your favourite dish?
> – *Look ahead to chapter 8 to talk about food and drink.*

Qu'est-ce que tu préfères boire?
Je préfère boire …
Ma boisson préférée est …

A quelle heure préfères-tu manger le soir?
Je préfère manger à sept heures.

Qu'est-ce que tu n'aimes pas manger?
Je n'aime pas / Je déteste manger …

> – *It's a good idea, and much more interesting, to talk about the things you really like eating, although you need to know how to say what you don't like, as well.*

POSITIVE ☺	NEGATIVE ☹

J'adore la moutarde.
Je préfère …
J'aime beaucoup …
C'est délicieux …
C'est super.
C'est savoureux (tasty).
Ça sent bon. (It smells good.)
C'est bon pour la santé.
	Je deteste la moutarde.
	Je n'aime pas …
	Je ne mange pas de viande.
	Je ne bois pas de vin.
	C'est trop sucré / salé.
	  (It's too sweet / salty.)
	Ça me donne mal au coeur.
	  (It makes me feel sick.)
	Je n'aime pas le goût.
	C'est mauvais pour la santé.

– *To talk about what you did last night* hier soir *or this morning* ce matin *you need to put verbs into the perfect tense (e.g. ate, drank). (Mind Map page 122.)*

3 Qu'est-ce que tu as fait ce matin?   = What did you do this morning?

Ce matin je **me suis réveillé(e)** à sept heures.

Puis, je **me suis lavé(e)** et je **me suis habillé(e)**.

Après, je **suis descendu(e) dans la cuisine** où j'**ai pris** mon petit déjeuner. **J'ai mangé** des céréales et j'**ai bu** du thé. **J'ai quitté** la maison à huit heures.   *– See page 141 for a revision of the perfect tense.*

– *To talk about what you will do tonight* ce soir, *tomorrow* demain *or next week* la semaine prochaine, *put the verbs into the future tense (e.g. will eat, will drink). See the Mind Map on page 124.*

Que feras-tu demain soir?   = What will you do tomorrow evening?

Demain soir j'**arriverai** chez moi à cinq heures. Je **regarderai** la télévision puis je **prendrai** le dîner. Après je **ferai** la vaisselle et je **ferai** mes devoirs. A neuf heures je **regarderai** la télévision ou j'**écouterai** mes disques. Puis à dix heures je **prendrai** une douche et je me **coucherai**.   *– See page 143 for a revision of the future tense.*

– *Listen for the time markers such as* hier *or* demain *and use the appropriate tense!*

4 Je peux t'aider?   = Can I help you? (to a friend)

Je peux te donner un coup de main?

Je peux vous aider?   = Can I help you? (to an older person)

Je peux aider à faire la vaisselle?   = Can I help do the washing up?

There's a brilliant Mind Map on page 97 about all the jobs that need doing at home. You will need to be able to talk about all the rotten chores – even if you never do them!

5 Qu'est-ce que tu dois faire chez toi?   = What do you have to do at home?
Je dois ranger ma chambre.   = I have to tidy my room.

Et les autres?   = And the others?

Ma soeur doit faire la vaisselle tous les jours.   *– Add extra detail such as* tous les jours / deux fois par semaine *wherever you can.*

Ce n'est pas juste!   = It's not fair!

C'est trop!   = It's too much!

Ce n'est pas assez!   = It's not enough!

Je fais plus / que lui / qu'elle!   = I do more than him / her!

A mon avis, il / elle est paresseux / paresseuse.   = In my opinion, he / she is lazy.

Il devrait faire la vaisselle plus souvent.   = He ought to wash up more often.

6 Tu partages ta chambre?   = Do you share your bedroom?

Oui je partage ma chambre avec ma soeur.

Non j'ai une chambre à moi.

Non j'ai ma propre chambre.

J'ai une chambre propre.   propre *before the noun* = own
propre *after the noun* = clean

Going for an A?

Revise the conditional tense (see page 144) then try the Test yourself tasks. The writing activity practises the use of the conditional tense. Remember that the examiners reward tenses other than the present, perfect and future as well as expressions such as the ones in the Checklist. Don't forget to learn the parts of the verbs in the conditional tense which allow you to describe the actions of other people, for example: il / elle voudrait, ils / elles aimeraient.

Try to talk for a minute about how you help out at home. For example, say which jobs you do and how you feel about doing them; which rooms you do each job in and at what time of day. When you know what you're going to say, set about recording yourself and then play it back to check how you sound.

If you get stuck for things to say, remember that you can comment on what people do **not** do. For example:

Mon frère **ne** fait **pas** la vaisselle – ce **n**'est **pas** juste.

Test yourself

Task 1

Write between 100 – 120 words on **Ma chambre idéale**.

j'aimerais = I would like	j'aimerais acheter = I would like to buy
je voudrais = I would like	il y aurait = there would be
j'aimerais avoir = I would like to have	

Add why you would like to have or buy something, and use lots of adjectives about colour, size, etc. When you've written it, ask your teacher to check your work for accuracy. Remember to thank him / her!

Task 2

Have a go at this cassette exercise (Side 1, Chapter 2). Play it twice.

Les tâches ménagères

Ecoutez les trois jeunes. Cochez (✓) la case Vrai ou la case Faux.

			Vrai	Faux
Pierre	1	Pierre fait la cuisine tous les jours.	☐	☐
	2	Le soir, il nettoie les poubelles.	☐	☐
	3	Pierre aide plus que son frère, Yves.	☐	☐
Christelle	1	Le soir, Christelle passe l'aspirateur.	☐	☐
	2	Anne aide à faire la cuisine.	☐	☐
	3	Anne n'aide pas assez.	☐	☐
Paul	1	Paul ne fait rien chez lui.	☐	☐
	2	Le soir, Pascale met le couvert.	☐	☐
	3	Les parents de Paul pensent qu'il n'aide pas assez.	☐	☐

Answers

TASK 2
Pierre – 1F 2F 3V; **Christelle** – 1F 2V 3F;
Paul – 1F 2F 3V.

Remember to look back at the Checklist. Well done – you've finished the chapter!

3

Mes passe-temps

Time out for leisure

This could be one of your favourite subjects, so make the most of it and enjoy using the vocabulary and phrases. The Mind Maps on pages 100 – 103 will help you learn all the material for giving opinions about a film, discussing sports and hobbies and the things you like most.

Help is at hand!

Notes/Options

1 Qu'est-ce que tu fais pendant ton temps libre?

Look up the Mind Map on page 100 and visualise yourself doing each activity while saying the French expression. That way you're more likely to remember!

Je fais du vélo, je sors avec mes amis.	
Je joue au tennis et je nage.	
jouer au foot	= to play football
jouer au basket	= to play basketball
Je nage	
Je lis, j'aime les livres de science-fiction et je lis des magazines.	je lis = je fais de la lecture
Je joue du piano.	= I play the piano.
Je joue de la guitare.	= I play the guitar.
Je vais au cinéma / au club des jeunes.	
Je fais partie d'un orchestre / d'un groupe.	= I'm a member of an orchestra / a group.

checklist
What you need to know

Are you OK on leisure subjects?
In French, can you:

		Fine	Help!
1	understand and give details about your interests and how you spend your free time (hobbies, sports, clubs, music)?	●	●
2	say how long you have had your interests?	●	●
3	give simple opinions about your activities, and say why you like or dislike doing certain things?	●	●
4	ask what a friend does?	●	●
5	ask what a friend would like to do?	●	●
6	ask for and give information about when activities start and finish?	●	●
7	arrange to meet at a certain time and place?	●	●
8	buy tickets for pool, sports ground, leisure activities?	●	●
9	apologise for being late?	●	●
10	say what kind of films and TV programmes you watch?	●	●
11	say how you spend your pocket money?	●	●
12	say what there is to do in the area where you live?	●	●
13	say what you did recently (such as last weekend)?	●	●
14	say what you plan to do (such as next weekend)?	●	●

2 Depuis combien de temps est-ce que tu fais ça? Depuis un an / depuis deux ans. = How long have you been doing that? = For one / two years.

3 Ça te plaît la natation? Tu aimes la natation? Oui j'aime beaucoup la natation. = Do you like swimming? j'aime = I like j'adore = I really like

Tu aimes jouer de la guitare? Oui j'adore jouer de la guitare. = Do you like playing the guitar?

Pourquoi?

Je joue bien et j'aime la musique. C'est intéressant. = I play well and I like music. It's interesting.

Tu es sportif / sportive? = Are you fond of sport? sportif = *masculine* sportive = *feminine*

Non je ne suis pas sportif / sportive.

Je n'aime pas le sport. Je ne joue pas bien et c'est fatigant. = tiring

Tu aimes la musique?

Oui j'adore la musique pop.

J'aime le rock. Mon groupe préféré s'appelle … = My favourite group is called …

4 Que fais-tu pendant ton temps libre? = What do you do in your free time?

5 Que veux-tu faire ce soir / samedi? = What would you like to do this evening / on Saturday?

– *If you want to ask a friend if he or she would like to do a particular thing use* tu veux + *infinitive. (See page 146.)*

Tu veux …? … nager … sortir … jouer au tennis = Do you want …? = … to go swimming = … to go out = … to play tennis

– *If you want to suggest going somewhere, you use:*

Tu veux aller + à la piscine? = to the swimming-pool?

Tu veux aller + au cinéma = to the cinema?

Si on allait + aux magasins? = to the shops?

6 … commence à quelle heure? le film la pièce le concert le match = When does the … start? = film = play = the concert = the match

La séance commence à huit heures. = The performance starts at 8 pm.

A quelle heure finit le film? à quelle heure? = at what time?

Le film finit à dix heures du soir. finit = finishes du soir = in the evening

– *Starting and finishing times might need the 24-hour clock; so remember 7 pm = 19 heures.*

7 On se rencontre à … = We'll meet at …

The Mind Map on page 103 will help you memorise names of places to go to and times!

c'est trop tôt = that's too early	c'est trop tard = that's too late
d'accord = that's fine	Ça va? = Is that all right?

c'est trôp tot

c'est trop tard

Ça va?

d'accord

8 Je voudrais une place . . .
... au balcon
... à l'orchestre

une place = a seat
= in the balcony
= in the stalls

Je voudrais un billet.

= I'd like a ticket.

9 Je suis désolé(e), je suis
en retard!

= I'm sorry, I'm late!

10 Tu regardes souvent la
télévision?

Oui je regarde la télévision
tous les soirs.

tous les soirs = every
evening

Quelle sorte d'émissions
préfères-tu?

Je préfère ...

Memorise vocabulary for the different
types of TV programmes and practise
giving reasons why you like or dislike them!
See page 102. Examiners love enthusiasm!

Tu vas souvent au cinéma?

Je vais au cinéma une fois
par mois.

une fois = once
par mois = a month
(per month / monthly)

Quelle sorte de films
préfères-tu?

11 On te donne de l'argent de
poche?

= Do you get pocket
money?

Je reçois 25 francs par
mois / par semaine.

= I get 25 francs a
month / a week.

Non, je gagne de l'argent.

= No, I earn money.

Est-ce que tu dépenses
ton argent de poche?

tu dépenses = you
spend

Oui, j'achète des magazines
et des vêtements.

= Yes, I buy
magazines and clothes.

12 Qu'est-ce qu'il y a à faire
pour les jeunes dans ta
ville?

= What is there for
young people to do in
your town?

Il y a un cinéma, un centre
de loisirs, une piscine et
une discothèque.

On peut aller au cinéma,
faire du sport, nager et aller
à la discothèque.

– **On peut** + *infinitive*
= *one can / you* **can**
+ *activity.*

13 Qu'est-ce que tu as fait le
week-end dernier?

Activities (perfect tense)
j'ai joué = I played
j'ai vu un film = I saw a film
je suis allé(e) = I went
je suis sorti(e) = I went out
j'ai fait du vélo = I went on a bike ride
je me suis bien amusé(e) = I enjoyed myself

Revise the perfect tense (pages 141–2) so
that you can talk about what you did in the
past, such as last weekend. See page 101.

Time markers – use perfect tense	
samedi dernier	= last Saturday
hier soir	= last night
la semaine dernière	= last week

More time markers – use future tense	
ce soir	= this evening
demain (soir)	= tomorrow (evening)
samedi prochain	= next Saturday
ce week-end	= this weekend
le week-end prochain	= next weekend

14 Qu'est-ce que tu vas faire
ce week-end?

Remember the two ways to talk about future plans?

A Use **je vais** + infinitive.

Je vais sortir. = I am going to go out.
Je vais aller au cinéma. = I am going to go to the cinema.
Je vais jouer au tennis. = I am going to play tennis.

B Use the future tense (see pages 124 and 143).

Activities (future tense)
je jouerai = I will play
je verrai = I will see
j'irai = I will go
je sortirai = I will go out
je ferai du vélo = I will go on a bike ride
je m'amuserai = I will have a good time

Going for a C?

'Pad out' your descriptions of the activities you do. For example, say when and how often you do things. And remember to say why you like certain things. Have another look back at the Notes/Options 13 and 14.

Ecrivez à une amie française, Amina. Décrivez ce que vous avez fait le week-end dernier. (100 mots)

Notice the time marker **dernier** – this points to the past! Remember to use the perfect tense.

– In your written work examiners will look for what you have to say (communication) as well as the way you say it (accuracy). Check your work for communication by looking at the Mind Maps.

– Make sure you understand the question before you start, use a dictionary to check. Vital words are the time markers as they give you clues about which time zone you are in and which tense you need (future, perfect or present).

You can check spellings with dictionaries and with the Mind Maps but you may need further help from a teacher.

Look at this answer.

Gloucester

le 7 mai

Chère Amina,

J'espère que tu vas bien. J'ai passé un très bon week-end. Vendredi, je suis sortie avec mes amis. Je suis allée au cinéma et j'ai vu un film d'aventure. C'était chouette. Samedi je me suis levée à 11 heures. L'après-midi, j'ai nagé à la piscine et samedi soir je suis allée à une boum chez Paul. J'ai dansé et j'ai bavardé. Je me suis bien amusée.

Hier, j'ai fait du vélo à la campagne (c'était fatigant!) et hier soir j'ai écouté un nouveau CD puis j'ai regardé la télévision.

Ecris-moi vite!

Amitiés

Eli

Check through your answer and highlight all the verbs in the perfect tense. Then learn them all!

Remember only girls add the extra 'e': je suis sorti(e), je suis allé(e).

TAKE A BREAK

Now try the Test yourself exercises! When you've done them, look back at the Checklist on page 25 – you should now be feeling fine for all of the questions.

Test yourself

Task 1

Lisez les descriptions des passe-temps.

Marc

Je fais de la natation et je joue souvent au foot – j'adore ça. Je suis très sportif.

Anne

Moi, j'aime beaucoup la musique, j'adore écouter des CD et je vais souvent au cinéma.

Julie

Je fais du cheval le samedi et le dimanche je sors – je fais du vélo avec mes amis. C'est génial.

Xavier

Le soir je joue avec mon ordinateur et je joue de la guitare – je fais partie d'un groupe. J'aime lire aussi.

Regardez les dessins:

a    b

c    d

e    f

g    h

i    j

Indiquez les passe-temps de Marc, Anne, Julie et Xavier.

Exemple: Marc   a + g

Anne   _____ + _____

Julie   _____ + _____

Xavier   _____ + _____ + _____

Task 2

Go through the checklist and the Notes/Options with a friend. See how long you can talk about your interests. Use written prompts such as **le soir**, **le week-end**, **le sport** to jog your memory.

Can you talk for one minute?

Task 3

Ecrivez une liste de vos passe-temps, 1 – 10.

Exemple 1. Je regarde la télévision. Try to write out ten things! Use the Mind Maps on pages 100 and 103 to help you to check.

If you've got more than six things – that's great!

Task 4

Ecrivez une lettre (60 – 80 mots). Décrivez ce que vous faites d'habitude le week-end et le soir.

Use the present tense and time markers such as **d'habitude** and **normalement**.

Ask a friend to read the letter and give you a point for everything he or she understands. For example: Je vais au cinéma = 1 point. You should aim for six points.

TASK 1
Anne i + j   **Julie** h + d   **Xavier** e + b + c

Answers

29

Mes passe-temps

checklist
What you need to know

**Are you OK on leisure subjects?
In French, can you:**

	Fine	Help!

1 answer the questions on the
Foundation Checklist on
page 25?

*If you've ticked the Help! box, go back to the
Foundation Notes/Options and revise!*

2 understand and give
preferences and opinions
about your hobbies and
activities (and those of other
people)?

3 discuss and give opinions
about films and TV
programmes?

4 say what you would like to
do if you had the money and
the time?

Time out for leisure

This could be one of your favourite subjects, so make the most of it and enjoy using the vocabulary and phrases. The Mind Maps on pages 100 – 103 will help you learn all the material for giving opinions about a film, discussing sports and hobbies and the things you like most.

Help is at hand!

Notes/Options

1 *Having looked back at the Foundation Checklist, do you feel really confident? If so, then carry on!*

2 Quel est ton passe-temps préféré?

préféré = favourite

Je préfère jouer au tennis.

– You need an infinitive after je préfère.

Je préfère faire de la voile.

faire de la voile = sailing

Mon passe-temps préféré –

c'est faire de la voile.

3 Que penses-tu de . . . ?

The Mind Map on page 102 will help you give your opinions here.

4 Que ferais-tu si tu avais beaucoup d'argent et beaucoup de temps libre?

Si j'avais beaucoup d'argent et beaucoup de temps libre j'irais …

= If I had lots of money

j'irais = I would go

j'achèterais = I would buy

je jouerais = I would play

je ferais beaucoup de sport = I would do a lot of sport

Going for an A?

Revise the conditional tense on page 144.

Be ready to give your opinion and say why you have that opinion!

The following opinions are mixed up! Make up two lists, one positive (**c'est cool!**) and one negative (**c'est moche!**) Use a dictionary to help if you get stuck.

1 ça élimine le stress
2 ça me change les idées
3 c'est ennuyeux
4 c'est une perte de temps
5 ce n'est pas cher
6 ça m'intéresse
7 c'est bête
8 c'est trop cher
9 c'est bon pour la santé
10 c'est sans intérêt
11 c'est bien de rester entre copains
12 ça (me) détend
13 ça me stresse
14 c'est génial
15 c'est reposant
16 ça prend trop de temps
17 c'est fatigant

Now say what you like / dislike doing (see the Mind Map on page 100 for lots of ideas) and link it to a **cool** or **moche** expression! These might be useful:

j'adore faire du sport
ça me détend
ça élimine le stress
c'est bon pour la santé

Test yourself

Task 1

Prepare a talk – 1–2 minutes long.

Try to say at least two things on each point and remember to give preferences and reasons why. Use the following cues:

Mes activités
le soir / le week-end
quand? souvent?
avec qui? où?
préférences? pourquoi?

You'll also find the Plan useful on page 32.

Task 2

This is a cassette exercise (side 1, Chapter 3 Higher). Listen twice.

Cécile et Marc vont au cinéma.

Cochez (✓) la case Vrai ou la case Faux:

	Vrai	Faux
Exemple: Cécile voudrait aller au cinéma ce soir.	☐	✓ (c'est faux)

Ecoutez la conversation.

	Vrai	Faux
1 Cécile adore les films d'amour.	☐	☐
2 Marc voudrait voir un film d'horreur.	☐	☐
3 La soeur de Marc a déjà vu 'Sept jours au Tibet'.	☐	☐
4 Marc dit que les images du film sont impressionantes.	☐	☐
5 Marc et Cécile vont se rencontrer à huit heures et quart.	☐	☐
6 Marc et Cécile vont se rencontrer au café.	☐	☐
7 Après le film, ils vont rentrer en taxi.	☐	☐

3

Ecrivez un article (120 mots) sur les loisirs et les jeunes dans ta ville.

Plan

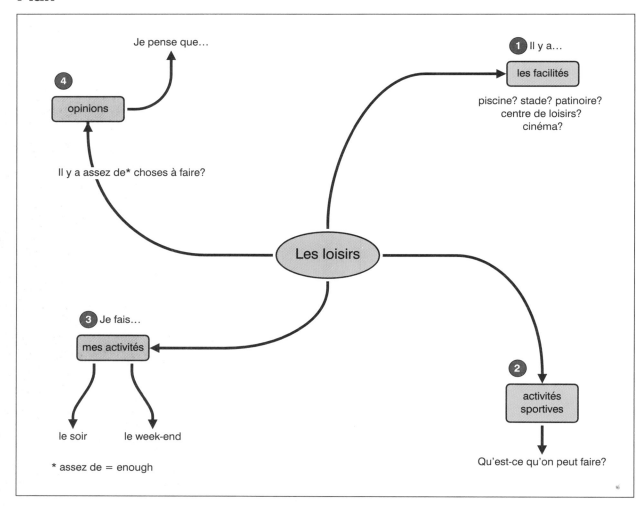

Je pense que…

4 opinions

Il y a assez de* choses à faire?

1 Il y a…

les facilités

piscine? stade? patinoire?
centre de loisirs?
cinéma?

Les loisirs

3 Je fais…

mes activités

le soir   le week-end

* assez de = enough

2 activités sportives

Qu'est-ce qu'on peut faire?

TAKE A BREAK

4

En vacances

Where are you staying?

One of the most important aspects about using Mind Maps to learn a language is that you master the skill of word association. For example, don't just learn the word for hotel facilities. You should picture and find out the words for each facility you can think of, or find on the Mind Map. Be creative and feel free to link up the Mind Maps between chapters and let your mind associate words and chapters in any direction.

Help is at hand!

Notes/Options

1 Bonjour Monsieur / Madame, je m'appelle . . .

j'ai fait une réservation pour ma famille.	= I've made a reservation for my family.
j'ai téléphoné pour réserver des chambres.	= I phoned to reserve rooms.
j'ai écrit pour réserver des chambres.	= I wrote to reserve rooms.

You'll find the Mind Map on page 104 useful at this stage.

2

Vous avez des chambres pour ce soir?	= Have you got any rooms for tonight?
Vous avez de la place pour ce soir?	= Have you any space for tonight?
Vous avez une chambre pour deux personnes?	= Have you got a double room?
Vous avez une chambre pour une personne?	= Have you got a single room?

checklist
What you need to know

How much can you say about holiday accommodation? In French, can you:

		Fine	Help!
1	check in, say who you are and say a reservation has been made?	●	●
2	ask what rooms are available?	●	●
3	give details, such as kind of room, length of stay?	●	●
4	ask the cost?	●	●
5	ask to see the room?	●	●
6	ask about the facilities?	●	●
7	ask about keys and leaving / returning times to the hotel?	●	●
8	ask about meals (times, availability)?	●	●
9	say you want to pay the bill?	●	●
At a youth hostel			
10	ask to hire a sleeping bag?	●	●
11	understand hostel rules?	●	●
At a campsite			
12	ask for space for a tent or a caravan?	●	●
13	ask about facilities?	●	●
14	ask about rules?	●	●
General			
15	make a simple complaint (such as lack of hot water)?	●	●
16	write a booking letter and understand the reply?	●	●
17	ask for details about a town or region you want to visit?	●	●

3 Je voudrais une chambre
pour moi-même.
Je voudrais une chambre
pour mes parents / mes amis.

moi-même = myself

C'est pour une nuit. = It's for one night.

Je voudrais une chambre avec
téléphone.
grand lit
douche
salle de bains
balcon
vue sur mer

= I'd like a room with
a phone.
= double bed
= a shower
= a bathroom
= a balcony
= a seaview

4 C'est combien une chambre?

= How much is a
room?

Ça fait combien par nuit? par nuit = per night

C'est trop cher! = It's too expensive!

Le petit déjeuner est compris? = Is breakfast
included?

5 Je peux voir la chambre
s'il vous plaît?

= Can I see the room,
please?

The Mind Map on page 104 should be useful
for memorising the vocabulary at the hotel.

6 Est-ce qu'il y a un parking
à l'hôtel?
un ascenseur

= Is there a car park
in the hotel?
= a lift

Est-ce qu'il y a un téléphone
dans la chambre?
un sèche-cheveux

= Is there a phone in
the room?
= a hair-dryer

7 Je peux avoir la clé? = Can I have the key?

C'est quelle chambre? = Which room is it?

C'est la chambre 210 au
deuxième étage.

= It's room 210 on
the 2nd floor.

L'hôtel ferme à quelle heure? = When does the
hotel close?

Je peux avoir une clé pour la
porte d'entrée?

= Can I have a front
door key?

Vous tapez un code pour
entrer.

= You have to key in
a code to get in.

8 Le petit déjeuner est à quelle
heure?

= What time is
breakfast?

Je voudrais la demi-pension. = I'd like half board.

On sert le dîner à partir de 19
heures jusqu'à 21 heures 30.

= Dinner is served
from 7 – 9.30 pm.

9 Je voudrais payer s'il vous
plaît.

= I'd like to pay
please.

Je peux avoir la note s'il
vous plaît?

= Please can I have
the bill?

Vous acceptez les cartes
de crédit?

= Do you accept
credit cards?

10 Je peux louer un sac de
couchage?
une couverture

= Can I hire a
sleeping bag?
= a blanket

la salle à manger = the dining room

le dortoir = the dormitory

Où est le dortoir pour
garçons / filles?

= Where is the boys'
/ girls' dormitory?

Voici ma carte (de membre). = Here is my
(membership) card.

Où sont les lavabos? = Where are the
washbasins?

Où sont les WC? = Where are the
toilets?

Est-ce qu'il y a une tâche
à faire?

= Is there a job to do?

See the Mind Map on page 105 to check that
you know the tasks you might be asked to do.

11 Vous êtes priés de ... = You are requested
to ...

Il est interdit (de manger
dans le dortoir).

= It is forbidden (to
eat in the dormitory). /
No eating in the
dormitory

La porte est fermée à
11 h du soir.

= The door is closed
at 11 pm.

L'auberge ferme à 23 h. = The hostel closes
at 11 pm.

12 Au camping = At the campsite

Je voudrais un emplacement pour une tente. = I'd like a plot for a tent?

une caravane = a caravan

Vous êtes combien? = For how many people?

On est cinq, deux adultes et trois enfants. = There are five of us, two adults and three children.

une place = a plot
un emplacement = a plot
à l'ombre = in the shade
sous les arbres = under the trees
loin de la discothèque = a long way from the disco
près du lac = near the lake

13 Est-ce qu'il y a une piscine? = Is there a swimming-pool?

une alimentation = a food shop
une boulangerie = a baker's

14 Est-ce qu'on peut allumer un feu? = Can I / we light a fire?

Est-ce qu'on peut faire un barbecue? = Can I / we have a barbecue?

Est-ce qu'il est interdit d'allumer un feu? = Is it forbidden to light a fire?

Il faut laisser la voiture au parking après dix heures du soir. = You have to leave the car in the car park after 10 pm.

Il est interdit de circuler après 22h. = You must not drive around after 10 pm.

15 Problèmes! A l'hôtel.

Excusez-moi Monsieur / Madame mais . . .

Il n'y a pas d'eau chaude. = There isn't any hot water.

Il n'y a pas de serviette. = There isn't a towel.

La télévision ne marche pas. = The television doesn't work.

Le chauffage ne marche pas. = The heating doesn't work.

La douche ne marche pas. = The shower doesn't work.

Il y a beaucoup de bruit. = There is a lot of noise.

La chambre n'est pas propre! = The room isn't clean!

16 Monsieur / Madame = Dear Sir / Madam
– *Never start a formal letter with* **Cher** *or* **Chère**! *These are equivalents of Dear, as in loved one.*

Veuillez agréer, Monsieur / Madame, l'expression de mes sentiments distingués. = Yours sincerely / faithfully,
– *This is the formal way of signing off. It appears flowery to us, but it is French style!*

Dans l'attente du plaisir de vous accueillir. = We look forward to welcoming you.
– *Note the formal signing off used often by hotels – don't use this one yourself.*

4

Je regrette mais on est complet.	= I am sorry but we are full.	**17** Qu'est-ce qu'il y a à faire / voir dans la ville / région?	= What is there to do / see in the town / region?

Going for a C?

Read the letter below and pay particular attention to learning the highlighted phrases. It would be a good idea to try to learn the booking letter by heart!

This letter can be adapted by putting in different rooms, requirements and dates. It could also be used to book in at a campsite (see the Notes/Options 12).

Bath
le 20 avril

Monsieur / Madame,

Je voudrais réserver[1] deux chambres à votre hôtel **à partir du** 8 août **au** 10 août[2]. Je voudrais une chambre **avec un grand lit**[3] avec douche et une chambre **à deux lits**[4] avec salle de bains.

Est-ce que vous pouvez m'indiquer vos prix[5] et **m'envoyer une brochure sur l'hôtel?**[6]

Est-ce qu'il y a[7] un restaurant à l'hôtel? **J'arriverai**[8] le 8 août à 17 h. **Je vous envoie des arrhes de** 200F.[9]

J'attends confirmation de votre part.[10]

Veuillez agréer, Monsieur / Madame, l'expression de mes sentiments distingués.

Michael Woods

1. I'd like to reserve
2. from + date / to + date
3. with a double bed
4. with two single beds
5. Can you let me know your prices?
6. and send me a brochure about the hotel.
7. Is there a
8. I'll be arriving
9. I'm sending a deposit of
10. I await your confirmation

- To book at a youth hostel for two boys and two girls you would need to ask: **Avez-vous de la place pour deux garçons et deux filles?** (*change details as necessary*). You would still need to give details of dates, times of arrival and you may want to ask questions about facilities (*see Notes/Options 12 and 13*).

Continued on next page

A reply from a hotel.

Hôtel du Parc
le 29 avril

Monsieur,

En réponse à votre lettre[1], dont nous vous remercions vivement, c'est **avec plaisir que nous vous confirmons votre réservation**[2] de deux chambres du 8 au 10 août.

Veuillez trouver ci-joint nos tarifs[3] et un dépliant sur l'hôtel. **Je confirme**[4] qu'il y a un restaurant à l'hôtel.

Nous avons bien reçu vos arrhes pour un montant de 200F[5].

Dans l'attente du plaisir de vous accueillir. Nous vous prions d'agréer, Monsieur, l'assurance de nos sentiments dévoués.

Sabrine Blanquet
Directrice

[1] In reply to your letter

[2] We are pleased to confirm your reservation

[3] Please find enclosed our prices

[4] I confirm

[5] We have received your deposit for the sum of 200F

Test yourself

Task 1

Ecrivez une lettre de réservation à un hôtel pour:

3 les prix?

4 des arrhes de 300F.

2 les dates 16 au 31 août

Remember to use the booking letter on page 36 for some help, and even copy phrases from it if you get stuck!

4

Task 2

Here's a role play exercise.

You are booking in at a French hotel.

1 Posez la question.

2 Dites ce que vous voulez.

3 Dites ce que vous voulez.

4 Dites ce que vous voulez.

5 Posez la question.

Now try the role play again changing the room details and number of nights. Ask if there is a TV in the room or a swimming-pool at the hotel.

Task 3

Ecrivez une lettre de réservation à un camping pour:

1

2

3 les dates 14 au 28 juillet.

4 les prix?

5

Remember to check back to the booking letter to see if you have used the main highlighted phrases correctly.

Task 4

Lisez cette annonce.

CAMPING LES CRIQUES * NN**

Piscine – Jeux d'enfants – Restaurant - Parking

Salle de télévision – Douches –
Emplacements à l'ombre – Boulangerie

Animaux non admis   68 emplacements (tentes)

Tel 68-12-73-96   1 avril – 30 septembre

Qu'est-ce qu'il y a au camping?

Cochez les cases appropriées (✓).

Exemple

Going for a C?

Listen to the cassette (Side 1, Chapter 4 Foundation). Listen twice.

Ecoutez la conversation à l'hôtel. Notez les détails en français et cochez les cases appropriées. Ecoutez la cassette deux fois.

Réservation

1 NOM ....

2 Détails des chambres: 2 chambre(s)

   Une chambre avec................. lit(s)

   Une chambre avec .... lit(s)

3 Salle de bains ou douche? ....

4 Pour .... nuits.

5 Restaurant: ouvert de .... h à

   .... h ....

6 Piscine: ouvert de .... h à

   .... h ....

7 Terrain de jeux: oui ☐ non ☐

8 Parking – où? ....

9 Numéros des chambres .... et ....

TAKE A BREAK!

Now look back at the Checklist on page 33 – you should now be feeling Fine for all of the questions. If not spend ten minutes looking at the Mind Maps on pages 104–5 – then try to make your own Mind Map.

En vacances

4

checklist
What you need to know

How much can you say about holiday accommodation? In French, can you:

	Fine	Help!
1 answer the questions on the Foundation Checklist on page 33?		

If you've ticked the Help! box, go back to the Foundation Notes/Options and revise!

At a hotel

2 cope with more unexpected elements, such as mistaken identity, incorrect reservation details, losing a key, accidents in the room?		
3 make more detailed complaints, such as about the lack of facilities or too much noise?		
4 write a letter of complaint to a hotel and explain the problem?		

Where are you staying?

One of the most important aspects about using Mind Maps to learn a language is that you master the skill of word association. For example, don't just learn the word for hotel facilities. You should picture and find out the words for each facility you can think of, or find on the Mind Map. Be creative and feel free to link up the Mind Maps between chapters and let your mind associate words and chapters in any direction.

Help is at hand!

Notes/Options

1 *Check back to the Foundation Checklist. If you feel confident carry on!*

2 Vous vous êtes trompé(e). | = You have made a mistake.

Je ne suis pas M. Brown. Je suis M. Woods. | I'm not Mr Brown. I'm Mr Woods.

J'ai réservé deux chambres la semaine dernière. | = I reserved two rooms last week.

Je voulais une chambre avec douche. | = I wanted a room with a shower.

Je voulais seulement une chambre. | = I wanted only one room.

Je vous ai écrit – voici votre lettre de confirmation. | = I wrote to you, here is your letter of confirmation.

Je vous ai envoyé un fax. | = I sent you a fax.

J'ai déjà versé des arrhes. | = I've already paid a deposit.

La note n'est pas correcte. | = The bill is wrong.

J'ai perdu ma clé – Je suis désolé(e). | = I've lost my key, I'm sorry.

J'ai cassé la lampe / la télévision. | = I've broken the lamp / TV.

J'ai renversé du lait / du vin.　= I've spilt some milk / some wine.

3 Je ne peux pas dormir – il y a trop de bruit.　= I can't sleep - there's too much noise.

J'ai eu froid hier soir. Il n'y avait pas de couvertures dans la chambre.　= I was cold last night. There were no blankets in the room.

L'eau est froide.　= The water is cold.

4 Le service était affreux.　= The service was awful.

Les garçons n'étaient pas polis.　= The waiters were impolite.

Les repas étaient froids.　= The meals were cold.

Le chauffage ne marchait pas.　= The heating wasn't working.

Il y avait beaucoup de bruit.　= There was a lot of noise.

La salle de bains était sale.　= The bathroom was dirty.

J'espère que vous ne tarderez pas à me rembourser une partie du prix de séjour.　= I hope that you will not delay in repaying part of the cost to me.

Going for an A?

Read this letter making sure you understand all of the points and then you can memorise the key phrases.

A letter of complaint

> 6 Waterborne Road
> LONDON
> SW17 4JP
>
> le 29 août
>
> Monsieur Casé
> Directeur
> Hôtel de la Place
>
> Monsieur,
>
> J'ai le regret de vous informer que je ne suis pas du tout satisfait(e) de mon séjour à votre hôtel (du 20 au 23 août). Le service était affreux – au restaurant, les garçons n'étaient pas très polis et les repas étaient froids.
>
> J'ai passé une nuit très fatigante dans ma chambre. Le chauffage ne marchait pas et à cause d'une soirée disco à l'hôtel il y avait beaucoup de bruit. La salle de bains était sale et j'ai dû demander une serviette propre.
>
> J'espère que vous ne tarderez pas à me rembourser une partie du prix de séjour.
>
> Veuillez agréer, Monsieur, mes salutations distinguées
>
> Alex Hanson.

Test yourself

Task 1

Listen to the cassette (Side 1, Chapter 4 Higher). Play it twice.

Ecoutez les quatre conversations.

Pour chaque conversation (1 – 4) notez le problème en français.

Ecoutez la cassette deux fois.

Exemple 1 – le chauffage ne marche pas.

Task 2

Vous avez passé un mauvais séjour à un hôtel. Ecrivez une lettre (120 mots) au directeur / à la directrice. Décrivez les problèmes. Demandez un remboursement.

Use the model letter to help!

Check back to the letter and correct your mistakes.

Task 3

Read the following article which gives advice about what to do if your rented holiday accommodation is not up to standard. Answer the questions in English.

> Votre location de vacances ne vous convient pas? – La maison avec 'vue sur la mer' donne sur un parking et le trois-pièces n'est qu'un studio. Quels sont vos droits? Que faut-il faire?
>
> Dès votre arrivée faites la liste des éléments incorrects et adoptez une stratégie.
>
> Vous restez ... avec une réduction.
>
> • Demandez une réduction du prix de la location. Si le propriétaire vous fait la sourde oreille téléphonez à l'office du tourisme.
>
> • Adressez un courrier à la commission départementale de l'action touristique qui effectuera une visite de contrôle.
>
> • Si vous avez loué par l'intermédiaire d'un organisme (Gîtes de France ...) contactez le responsable qui trouvera un accord aimable avec le propriétaire.

> Vous partez: exigez d'être remboursé. Si vous partez demandez le remboursement des sommes déjà payées. Si vous avez versé des arrhes vous avez le droit de demander le double de la somme.
>
> Les négociations se passent mal? Avant de porter plainte auprès du Procureur de la République n'oubliez pas ...
>
> • que vous pouvez faire appel à un témoin.
>
> • de prendre des photos de la propriété pour faire valoir vos droits.
>
> • de faire une copie de votre contrat.

1 What should you do as soon as you arrive?

2 If you decide to stay, what should you ask the owner to do?

3 If the owner is uncooperative where should you ring for help?

4 If you rent a property through a company or agency (e.g: Gîtes de France), what should you do?

5 If you decide to leave, what should you ask the owner to do?

6 If you have given the owner a deposit, what can you ask for?

7 What should you do before you make a complaint to a public prosecutor (Procureur de la République)?

Answers

TASK 1
1 Le repas était froid - le service était affreux, les garçons étaient impolis.
2 La chambre est sale. Il n'y a pas de serviettes dans la salle de bains.
3
4 La note n'est pas correcte (le client n'a pas mangé à l'hôtel).

TASK 3
1 Make a list of things which aren't right.
2 Give you a reduction.
3 The Tourist Office.
4 Contact the person in charge at that agency / there.
5 Refund any money already paid.
6 Ask for double the amount of the deposit
7 Get a witness, take photos of the property, make a copy of the contract.

5 Mes vacances

Describing a holiday

This is another favourite topic of conversation! The Mind Maps on pages 106 – 7 will help you to memorise the key vocabulary about what you do on holiday, where you go and so on. Keep referring to the Mind Maps until you are confident of all the words and phrases, and have a go at drawing your own map based on your last holiday.

Help is at hand!

	Notes/Options
1 Tu as combien de semaines de vacances scolaires?	
J'ai deux semaines à Noël, une semaine pour les vacances du mi-trimestre, deux semaines à Pâques, une semaine en mai, six semaines pour les grandes vacances et une semaine en octobre.	Noël = Christmas mi-trimestre = half term Pâques = Easter
2 D'habitude où vas-tu en vacances?	d'habitude = normally
Normalement, je vais au bord de la mer. à la montagne à la campagne	= to the mountains = to the country
	– Remember to use the present tense. For example: je vais au bord de la mer.
Tu restes /descends à l'hôtel?	= Do you stay in a hotel?
Oui je descends à l'hôtel.	= Yes, I stay in a hotel.

checklist
What you need to know

How confident are you of these questions? In French, can you:

	Fine	Help!
1 say how many weeks' school holidays you have a year and name the holidays?		
2 say where you normally go on holiday?		
3 say who you go with?		
4 say for how long you go?		
5 say what you do on holiday?		
6 ask other people for the above information?		
7 say how you travel?		
Describe a recent holiday		
8 say where you went, who you went with and how you travelled?		
9 say what the weather was like?		
10 say what you did and saw?		
11 give simple opinions about the holiday?		
12 talk about holiday plans for your next holiday?		
13 ask for details about a town or region you want to visit as a tourist?		

Non, on loue un gîte ou un appartement.	= No, we hire a holiday cottage or a flat.
Non, je séjourne dans un appartment / une maison de vacances.	= No, I stay in a holiday flat / house.
Non je vais au camping.	= No I go to a campsite.
On va à l'auberge de jeunesse.	= We go to a youth hostel.
Non je fais du camping.	= No I go camping.
Tu restes en Angleterre ou tu vas à l'étranger? Je vais à l'étranger. Je vais en France / en Espagne.	à l'étranger = abroad

Look at the Mind Map on page 107.

Je vais à Paris / à Madrid.	– *Use à with the name of a town or city.*
Je reste en Angleterre. Je vais à Swanage.	= I stay in England. I go to Swanage.

3 Avec qui est-ce que tu pars en vacances? Je vais en vacances avec mes amis. Je pars en vacances avec ma famille.
	= Who do you go on holiday with?

4 Tu pars pour combien de temps? Je pars pour une semaine / huit jours.
une quinzaine	= a week = a fortnight
Pendant combien de temps?	= For how long?
Pendant deux semaines / quinze jours.	= For two weeks.

5 Que fais-tu pendant tes vacances?

See the Mind Map on page 106 for some more ideas.

Je fais de la natation, je joue au tennis et je vais à la plage.	
Je fais du shopping / du lèche-vitrines.	= I go shopping / window shopping.
Je me bronze / je visite la région.	= I sunbathe / I visit the region.
Je me promène / je fais des promenades.	= I go for walks.

6 Make sure you know all the questions from 1 to 4 on the Checklist so that you can ask other people about their holidays.

7 Comment voyages-tu?
	= How do you travel?
Je voyage en bateau.	= I travel by boat.
Je vais en avion. en voiture en train en car	= I travel by plane. = by car = by train = by coach
Le voyage prend combien de temps?	= How long does the journey take?
Le voyage dure …	= The journey lasts …
Ça prend cinq heures.	= It takes five hours.

– *All these Notes/Options require the present tense. However, remember to change the tense with different time markers such as **d'habitude** and **normalement**.*

For the following Notes/Options you need the perfect tense. (See page 122.)

8 Où es-tu allé(e) l'année dernière, pendant les grandes vacances?
	= Where did you go last year during the main / summer holidays?
Je suis allé(e) en France, au bord de la mer.	je suis allé(e) = I went
Tu es allé(e) avec qui?	= Who did you go with?
Tu es allé(e) en vacances avec tes ami(e)s? Non, je suis allé(e) avec ma famille.	= Did you go with your friends?
Tu es descendu(e) à l'hôtel?	=Did you stay at a hotel?

Non j'ai passé mes vacances dans un appartement.	= No, I spent my holiday in a flat.
Oui j'ai passé mes vacances à l'hôtel.	= Yes, I spent my holidays at a hotel.
Oui je suis descendu(e) à l'hôtel.	= Yes, I stayed at a hotel.
Comment as-tu voyagé?	
J'ai voyagé en bateau et en voiture.	j'ai voyagé = I travelled

9 Quel temps faisait-il pendant ton séjour?   = What was the weather like during your stay?

– *Note that **faisait** is a past tense – the imperfect tense. See the Grammar page 143 for more help on the imperfect.*

One of the Mind Maps on page 107 is all about the weather.

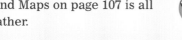

Il faisait beau / soleil / chaud / froid.	= The weather was fine / sunny / hot / cold.
Il pleuvait.	= It was rainy.
Il faisait de l'orage.	= The weather was stormy.

10 Qu'est-ce que tu as fait pendant les vacances?   = What did you do during the holidays?

J'ai nagé, j'ai joué au tennis et je suis sorti(e) avec mes amis.	= I swam, I played tennis and I went out with my friends.
Je me suis bronzé(e).	= I sunbathed.
J'ai fait la grasse-matinée.	= I got up late.
Je me suis promené(e).	= I went for walks.
J'ai acheté des souvenirs.	= I bought some souvenirs.

Qu'est-ce que tu as vu?

J'ai visité des monuments historiques, j'ai visité la ville et un parc de loisirs.

11 Qu'est-ce que tu as pensé de tes vacances?   What did you think of your holidays?

J'ai adoré les vacances.	= I loved my holidays.
Je me suis bien amusé(e).	= I had a good time.
J'ai aimé la nourriture et les gens.	= I liked the food and the people.
Je n'ai pas aimé la nourriture.	= I didn't like the food.

– *See the Higher section of this chapter for more opinions.*

Make sure you can ask the Checklist 7–12 so that you can ask other people what they did.

12 Quels sont tes projets de vacances pour cet été?   = What are your holiday plans for this summer?

Remember to talk about future plans, use either the future tense (see pages 124 and 143) or use **je vais** + the infinitive to say what you are going to do.

Look carefully at the Mind Map on page 106 so that you can handle the question in Notes/Options point 12.

13 Je voudrais des renseignements sur la ville.   = I would like some information about the town.

See Going for a C? on page 47.

Going for a C?

Remember, examiners will expect to hear what you do normally (present tense), what you did (perfect tense) and what you will do (future tense). Holidays is one of the best topics to show off how well you can do in the different time zones.

Record yourself reading out the Checklist from 1–7. Then record your answers.

Then do the same for 8–11.

Finally prepare your complete answer to 12 – as if you were in the exam!

Test yourself

Task 1

Use the cue card below and try to talk for about two minutes on **Mes vacances**.

Refer to the Notes/Options if you get stuck.

Mes vacances

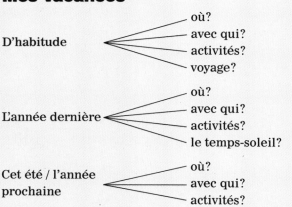

D'habitude
- où?
- avec qui?
- activités?
- voyage?

L'année dernière
- où?
- avec qui?
- activités?
- le temps-soleil?

Cet été / l'année prochaine
- où?
- avec qui?
- activités?

Task 2

Vous êtes en vacances. Ecrivez une carte postale (40 mots) à un(e) ami(e) en français.

Ecrivez:

1

2

3

4

Task 3

Répondez à cette lettre (100 mots).

le 2 septembre

Salut!

Comment vas-tu? As-tu passé de bonnes vacances? Où es-tu allé(e) et avec qui? Qu'est-ce que tu as visité?

Veux-tu venir en France à Noël? Je suis libre du 20 décembre au 3 janvier.

Réponds-moi vite.

Amitiés

Ame-Marie

Ask your teacher to check your work for accuracy. Don't be too ambitious – write only what you know how to say!

Remember to spot the questions in the letter; you must answer each question asked to get communication marks in the exam.

Going for a C?

How would you ask for details about a town or region you are planning to visit?

12 Fir Road
Hereford
Angleterre

le 5 mai

Syndicat d'Initiative
Collioure
France

Monsieur,

Je vous serais très obligé(e)[1] de m'envoyer[2] des informations sur la ville de Collioure. **Veuillez m'envoyer[3]** des brochures, un plan de la ville, une liste d'hôtels et une liste d'appartements à louer, s'il vous plaît. **Je voudrais aussi savoir[4] ce qu'il y a à faire[5]** dans la ville. Est-ce qu'il y a des monuments à visiter?

Veuillez trouver ci-joint une enveloppe pour la réponse.[6]

Je vous remercie d'avance.[7]

Veuillez agréer, Monsieur, l'expression de mes sentiments distingués.[8]

Sue Davidson

[1] I would be grateful if

[2] you could send me

[3] Please send me

[4] I would also like to know

[5] what there is to do?

[6] Please find enclosed an envelope for reply

[7] Thanking you in advance

[8] Yours faithfully

Test yourself

Task 4

Vous voulez visiter la ville de Béziers.
Ecrivez une lettre au Syndicat d'Initiative.

Demandez:

1 des brochures

2 un plan de la ville

3 ce qu'on peut visiter.

Posez des questions sur:

1 les jours de marché
2 les heures de fermeture des magasins

When you've finished check your letter back against the model letter on this page.

une brochure	= a brochure
un dépliant	= a leaflet
un plan	= a plan
une carte	= a map
une liste d'appartements à louer	= a list of flats to rent
une liste de restaurants	= a list of restaurants

Est-ce qu'il y a un musée?	= Is there a museum?
Qu'est-ce qu'on peut faire à Collioure?	= What can one do/is there to do in Collioure?
Quels sont les jours de marché?	= When are the market days?
Qu'est-ce qu'il y a à visiter?	= What is there to visit?
A quelle heure ferment les magasins?	= When do the shops close?
Quelle est la date de la fête régionale?	= When is the local festival day?

Mes vacances

5

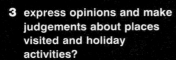

checklist
What you need to know

How confident are you of these questions? In French, can you:

                   Fine   **Help!**

1 answer the questions on the Foundation Checklist on page 43?

If you've ticked the Help! box, go back to the Foundation Notes/Options and revise!

2 give fuller details about places visited or holiday plans?

3 express opinions and make judgements about places visited and holiday activities?

Describing a holiday

This is another favourite topic of conversation! The Mind Maps on pages 106 – 7 will help you to memorise the key vocabulary about what you do on holiday, where you go and so on. Keep referring to the Mind Maps until you are confident of all the words and phrases, and have a go at drawing your own map based on your last holiday.

Help is at hand!

Notes/Options

1 *Once you've looked back at the Foundation Checklist on page 43 and you feel confident – carry on!*

2 Fuller details means that you must be able to give more than one or two factual details. You should be able to talk and write about your holidays in the past, present and future tenses using the correct time zone markers.

Perfect	Present	Future
L'année dernière …	D'habitude …. Normalement …	Cet été … L'année prochaine …
je suis allé(e)	je vais	j'irai
je suis resté(e)	je reste	je resterai
j'ai passé	je passe	je passerai
j'ai pris l'avion	je prends l'avion	je prendrai l'avion
je suis sorti(e)	je sors	je sortirai

Try continuing these three lists using verbs in the three tenses and draw your own Mind Maps for each time zone putting in the correct forms of the verbs. The Mind Maps on pages 122 – 24 will help you.

See Notes/Options 3 for more expressions.

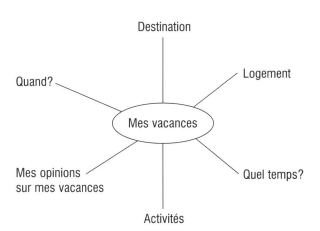

Destination

Quand?

Logement

Mes vacances

Mes opinions
sur mes vacances

Quel temps?

Activités

The difference between the Foundation cue card in Task 1
on page 46 and the above cue card is in the amount of
extra detail you can provide and the variety of verbs you
can use correctly without guidance from the examiner.

Going for an A?

Mes vacances idéales. Try to use the
conditional tense (see page 144) to
describe where you would spend your
dream holidays.

Start off
Si j'étais riche
Si j'avais beaucoup d'argent
Si j'avais assez de temps

j'irais	= I would go
je passerais un mois	= I would spend a month . . .
je resterais	= I would stay
je nagerais	= I would swim
je mangerais	= I would eat
je sortirais	= I would go out
je visiterais	= I would visit
je serais	= I would be

Remember that holidays and trips to
France are frequently discussed and tested
in examinations, so make sure that you can
cope with the different tenses.

Remember that examiners are looking for
opinions and reasons why.

3 Here are some useful
opinions about holiday trips
– some positive and some
negative. Use a dictionary to
help check the meanings if
you are stuck!

* Remember **parce que**
becomes **parce qu'il** before
a vowel.

POSITIVE	NEGATIVE
J'ai aimé mon séjour parce que / qu'	Je n'ai pas aimé mon séjour parce que / qu'
– c'était différent	– c'était ennuyeux
– c'était intéressant	– ce n'était pas intéressant
– la nourriture était délicieuse	– la nourriture était affreuse
– il faisait plus chaud qu'en Angleterre*	– il faisait trop chaud*
– les gens étaient sympa	– les gens n'étaient pas sympa
– les gens étaient accueillants	– les gens n'étaient pas accueillants
– j'étais souvent avec mes ami(e)s	– j'étais souvent avec mes parents(!)
– le paysage était très beau	– le paysage était sans intérêt
– j'ai visité beaucoup de choses	– j'ai visité trop de monuments

Test yourself

Task 1

Try recounting a school exchange trip to France; use the prompts to help.

Racontez l'histoire (3 minutes maximum).

"L'année dernière, je suis allé(e) en France avec le collège le 16 juillet …"

arriver à Douvres, passer par le péage
prendre le Shuttle
entrer dans le tunnel

partir du collège de bonne heure – comment? avec qui?

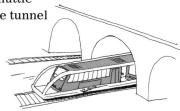

AUTOROUTE
prendre l'autoroute
passer 12 heures dans le car
voyage confortable?
quel temps faisait-il?

arriver en France?
à quelle heure? s'arrêter à Boulogne
descendre du car
prendre le petit-déjeuner.

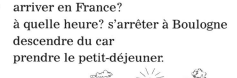

le 17 juillet
arriver à Béziers
rencontrer votre correspondant(e)
rentrer chez le / la
correspondant(e)
prendre le dîner en famille

le 20 juillet
aller à la plage – quel
 temps faisait-il?
rencontrer vos amis
qu'avez-vous fait?

le 26 juillet
repartir pour
l'Angleterre
vos réactions?

le 25 juillet
sortir à la discothèque
qu'avez-vous fait?
rentrer tard
vous étiez fatigué(e)?

le 22 juillet
visiter le château à Carcassonne
vos impressions?
acheter des souvenirs

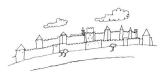

Now listen to the cassette (Side 1, Chapter 5 Higher) for a model answer.

6

Out and about

Make use of the signpost advice and look up the Mind Maps on pages 108 – 109. You'll find these most helpful not only for your exams, but also when you're travelling around France. Throughout this chapter, imagine yourself in all the situations and use the Mind Maps to be creative and expand on the phrases given.

Help is at hand!

Notes/Options

1 Décris-moi ta ville / ton village.

C'est une grande / petite ville.
il y a des usines

= there are factories

Elle est moderne / industrielle / historique / touristique / administrative.

Il y a des monuments historiques.

= There are historical monuments.

Où se trouve ta ville / ton village?

C'est dans le nord de l'Angleterre.

le sud / l'est / l'ouest

C'est à 100 kilomètres de Birmingham.

= It's 100 kilometres from Birmingham.

C'est à une heure de Leeds.

= It's an hour from Leeds.

Il y a quinze mille habitants.

= There are 15,000 inhabitants.

2 Qu'est-ce qu'il y a comme distractions dans ta ville?

= What kinds of leisure facilities are there in your town?

pour les jeunes
pour les touristes

= for young people
= for the tourists

Il y a	une piscine, un terrain de football, de grands magasins, un centre commercial, un jardin public, un parc, un théâtre, un cinéma, une bibliothèque, un centre sportif, des monuments historiques, une cathédrale

En ville

checklist
What you need to know

Can you:

		Fine	Help!
1	give a simple description of your home town and surrounding area?		
2	say what there is to do there (including festivals)?		
3	give simple opinions about your town?		
4	ask where a place is?		
5	say how to get to a place?		
6	understand directions given to you?		
7	give and understand information about public transport (bus, coach, train, underground)?		
8	understand simple signs and notices?		
9	buy tickets (destination, single / return, class)?		
10	buy fuel for a car and ask the cost?		
11	ask for the water, oil and tyres to be checked?		
12	give simple details about a breakdown?		
13	understand and describe weather conditions?		

| Qu'est-ce qu'on peut faire dans ta ville? | = What can one / you do in your town? |

– *Be prepared to talk about festivals in your town! For example:* Il y a un festival d'art / de danse / de musique. On chante et on danse.

| On peut | visiter les magasins
aller au festival de jazz
aller à la discothèque / aller au théâtre
faire du sport / des excursions
faire du tourisme |

3 Que penses-tu de ta ville?

POSITIVE
J'aime ma ville!
C'est intéressant! / C'est chouette!
Il y a beaucoup à faire.

NEGATIVE
Je n'aime pas ma ville!
C'est ennuyeux! / C'est moche!
Il n'y a rien à faire.

4 Où se trouve / est le jardin public?	= Where is the park?
la bibliothèque	= the library
le centre commercial	= the shopping centre

| **5/6** Pour aller à la gare s'il vous plaît? | = How do I get to the station, please? |

See the Mind Map on page 108 about how to get to places in a town. You could also visualise your own town along the same lines and draw a Mind Map of your neighbourhood.

Tournez à droite / à gauche.	= Turn to the right / left.
Continuez tout droit,	= Carry straight on,
prenez la première rue à droite	= take the first road on the right
traversez le pont.	= cross the bridge.
c'est après les feux / le rond-point.	= it's after the lights / the roundabout.
C'est loin? Non c'est près d'ici.	= Is it far? No it's nearby.
Prenez le bus numéro cinq, voilà l'arrêt d'autobus.	= Take the number five bus, there's the bus stop.

7 A quelle heure part le prochain train / car pour Paris?	= When does the next train / coach leave for Paris?
Il y un car pour Paris?	= Is there a coach to Paris?
A quelle heure arrive le train à Paris?	= When does the train arrive in Paris?
Le voyage prend combien de temps?	= How long does the trip take?
Ça prendra combien de temps?	= How long will it take?
Est-ce qu'il faut changer?	= Do I have to change trains?
C'est direct?	= Is it direct?
Il y a une correspondance?	= Is there a connection?
C'est quelle ligne? (métro)	= Which line is it? (underground)
la gare / la gare routière	= the railway / bus station
la station de métro	underground station
8 Attention!	= Watch out!

Many of the signs you see in France are obvious to English speakers.
Have a look at the Mind Map and signs on page 109 for the less obvious signs you need to know.

9 Buying a train ticket.

un aller-retour	= return ticket
un aller simple	= one-way ticket
en première classe / en deuxième classe	= in first / in second class
Ça coûte combien?	= How much is it?

> Je voudrais un aller-retour pour Paris.

> En quelle classe?

> En deuxième classe.

> C'est pour quel jour?

> C'est pour mardi prochain.

Je voudrais un carnet s'il vous plaît.

un carnet = a book of ten tickets
un ticket = one ticket.
Quel quai? = Which platform?

Le train part de quel quai? ⎱
De quel quai part le train? ⎰

= Which platform does the train leave from?

C'est quel quai?

Which platform is it?
le quai = la voie
– Both words can be used at a railway station.
la voie = the track

10 A la station service
Faites le plein s'il vous plaît.

= At the petrol station
= Fill it up, please.

Gazole ou essence?

le gazole = diesel
l'essence = petrol

Du super sans plomb.
avec plomb
ordinaire

= 4 star, unleaded
= leaded
= 2-star petrol

11 Vous désirez autre chose?

Oui un litre d'huile.	= Yes, a litre of oil.
Avez-vous une carte routière?	= Have you got a road map?
Où sont les toilettes?	= Where are the toilets?
Vous vendez des boissons?	= Do you sell drinks?
Voulez-vous vérifier les pneus / l'huile / l'eau?	= Would you check the tyres / oil / water?
C'est bien la route pour Dijon?	= Is this the right road to Dijon?

12 Je suis tombé(e) en panne.

= I've broken down (about a car!).

Le moteur ne marche pas.	= The engine isn't working.
Les freins ne marchent pas.	= The brakes aren't working.
J'ai crevé / un pneu est crevé.	= I've had a puncture.
C'est quelle marque de voiture?	= What make of car is it?
C'est une Ford.	= It's a Ford.
Quel est le numéro d'immatriculation?	= What is the registration number?
C'est R431 VMX.	*– Be prepared to give numbers and spell out the letters!*

Je suis à cinq kilomètres de Dijon.
une autoroute
une route nationale

= I'm five kilometres from Dijon.
= a motorway
= a main road (like an A-road)

13 Il pleut à verse! | It's pouring with rain!

For the complete scene on the weather front, look at the Mind Map on page 107. Describe your favourite weather and then your most dreaded weather.

Going for a C?

Learn the vocabulary below to help you understand weather forecasts.

agréable	= pleasant
une averse	= a shower
le climat	= the climate
la chute	= the drop (in temperature)
degré	= degree
demain	= tomorrow
un éclair	= a flash of lightning
une éclaircie	= a sunny spell
fort	= strong
léger	= light
meilleur	= better
la pluie	= the rain
plus tard	= later on
les prévisions	= forecasts
prochain	= next
rapidement	= quickly
la température	= the temperature
… basse / haute	= … low / high
Quel temps fait-il?	= What's the weather like?

Test yourself

Task 1

Cue card

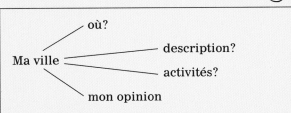

You should be getting really good at talking for one minute on a subject. Try talking about the town where you live.

Use the cue card and Notes/Options 1 – 3.

Task 2

Here's a role play exercise. Imagine that you are at Dijon railway station and want to go to Paris.

1

Le prochain train part à 11h 20.

2

Le train arrive à 13h.

3

D'accord, un aller simple à Paris en deuxième.

4

Ça fait 120 francs.

5

C'est quai No 3.

Task 3

This is a cassette exercise. Listen to Side 1, Chapter 6 Foundation. Play the cassette twice.

La météo

A

B

C

D

E

F

Choisissez la bonne image. Ecrivez la lettre dans la case.

Exemple: Le Nord | B |

1 La Région Parisienne | |

2 Le Languedoc | |

3 La Côte Atlantique | |

4 Les Alpes | |

Task 4

Choisissez la bonne letter (A – H) pour chaque numéro (1 - 6).

Exemple: Le buffet = B

1 Salle d'Attente =

2 Non fumeur =

3 Toilettes (femmes) =

4 Sortie =

5 Consigne =

6 Guichets =

A B

C D

E Billets F WC

G H

Task 5

Ecrivez une lettre (80 mots) à votre ami(e) français(e). Décrivez votre ville. Dites ce qu'il y a à faire. Dites ce que vous pensez de votre ville.

Use the Notes/Options to check your work.

Answers

TASK 2
1 A quelle heure part le prochain train pour Paris?
2 A quelle heure arrive le train à Paris?
3 Je voudrais un aller simple à Paris.
4 C'est combien?
5 C'est quel quai?

TASK 3
1 E, **2** F, **3** C, **4** D

TASK 4
1 G, **2** H, **3** F, **4** A, **5** C, **6** E

55

En ville

checklist
What you need to know

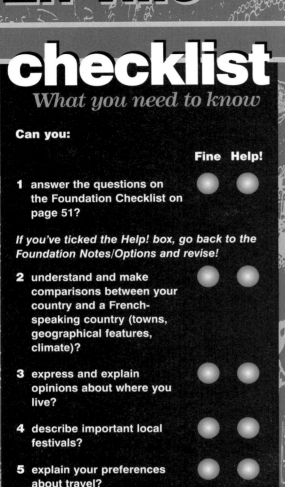

Can you:

	Fine	Help!
1 answer the questions on the Foundation Checklist on page 51?	○	○

If you've ticked the Help! box, go back to the Foundation Notes/Options and revise!

2 understand and make comparisons between your country and a French-speaking country (towns, geographical features, climate)?	○	○
3 express and explain opinions about where you live?	○	○
4 describe important local festivals?	○	○
5 explain your preferences about travel?	○	○
6 report an accident (giving location and details)?	○	○

Out and about

Make use of the signpost advice and look up the Mind Maps on pages 108 – 9. You'll find these most helpful not only for your exams, but also when you're travelling around in France. Throughout this chapter, imagine yourself in all the situations and use the Mind Maps to be creative and expand on the phrases given.

Help is at hand!

Notes/Options

1 *Once you've looked back at the Foundation Checklist and you feel confident – carry on!*

2

	plus … que = more than moins … que = less than
Le climat est plus / moins humide / sec qu'ici.	= The climate is more / less humid / dry than here.
chaud(e) froid meilleur	
Le paysage est plus / moins beau / vallonné.	= The countryside is more / less beautiful / hilly.
La région est plus / moins plate / verte.	= The region is more / less flat / green.
intéressant(e) montagneux(euse)	= interesting = mountainous

3 Quels sont les avantages et les inconvénients de ta ville?
J'aime / Je n'aime pas habiter chez moi …

parce qu'	il fait trop chaud / froid il y a beaucoup à faire il n'y a rien à faire il y a trop/de bruit / de pollution
parce que	j'habite trop loin des distractions / de mes amis le soir il n'y a pas de transport public - il est difficile de rentrer c'est une belle ville c'est une ville sans intérêt

4 la fête = a holiday / festival

la fête du village = the village fair

– *In France festivals are often associated with a religious day* – une fête religieuse.

Le premier mai c'était la fête du village. Il y avait un marché et le soir on a pris un grand repas. On a bien mangé, on a dansé et on a chanté – c'était chouette, on s'est bien amusé.

fêter	= to celebrate
un mariage	= a wedding
une boum	= a party
une pièce	= a play
un concert	= a concert
un spectacle	= a show
des feux d'artifice	= fireworks

5 Comment préfères-tu voyager?

Je préfere voyager	en avion en train en voiture en bus à vélo à pied	parce que	c'est rapide c'est confortable c'est pratique ce n'est pas cher c'est bon pour la santé

The Mind Map on page 108 will help you expand on what you already know.

6 Il y a eu un accident de route. = There's been a road accident.

On est sur la nationale 12 près de … = We're on the N12 near …

Un homme / le conducteur a été blessé. = A man / the driver has been hurt.

Il faut une ambulance. = An ambulance is needed.

Les voitures se sont percutées. = The cars crashed into each other.

La voiture a heurté un arbre / un camion. = The car crashed into a tree / a lorry.

La voiture est entrée en collision avec une moto. = The car crashed into a motorbike.

La voiture roulait trop vite. = The car was going too fast.

Le conducteur ne s'est pas arrêté. = The driver didn't stop.

Le conducteur a essayé de doubler. = The driver tried to overtake.

J'ai pris le numéro d'immatriculation. = I took the registration number.

L'accident s'est produit à dix heures. = The accident happened at 10 am.

Le conducteur n'a pas vu la moto. = The driver didn't see the motorbike.

Le conducteur a démarré sans regarder. = The driver started off without looking.

Il a brûlé les feux. = He went through the lights.

Il y avait beaucoup de circulation. = There was a lot of traffic.

C'était la faute du conducteur. = It was the driver's fault.

un témoin = a witness

Going for an A?

Faites une présentation de votre ville (sur cassette) pour un touriste français. Décrivez votre ville, les distractions et dites ce que vous pensez de votre ville.

- Remember, you should always try to give a reason for an opinion and link statements together using **parce que** – see Notes/Options 3 and 5 and learn the phrases. Use this cue card to express your opinions about the town where you live.

où   activités   description

ma ville

Test yourself

- At this level the examiners are looking for accuracy in written exercises and in particular the tenses. Task 1 concentrates on the present tense and Task 2 on the perfect and imperfect tenses. Make sure you are happy with these tasks; if you need help look at the grammar section.

Task 1

Où préférez vous habiter?
En ville ou à la campagne?
Dans votre pays ou à l'étranger?

Ecrivez 120 mots. Donnez vos raisons.

Use both the Foundation and Higher Notes/Options to check your work.

Task 2

Vous avez vu un accident de route en ville hier soir. Décrivez ce qui s'est passé. Ecrivez 150 mots.

- Remember to say where you were. For example: **J'étais dans la rue**. Also say what the weather was like; such as **Il pleuvait quand l'accident s'est produit**. (It was raining when the accident happened.)

Use phrases from the Notes / Options on page 57 (especially from 6) to help you.

Task 3

Lisez cet article.

Port-Vendres: la voiture a plongé par étourderie

Le spectaculaire plongeon d'une voiture, jeudi vers 19 heures, dans les eaux du port de Port-Vendres, n'était finalement pas dû à une fausse manoeuvre mais à une simple étourderie.

Une jeune femme de la région venait de garer son véhicule sur le quai de la Douane et était partie faire une course, oubliant de mettre le frein à main. Le temps de tourner le dos et l'auto a commencé à glisser avant de tomber dans le chenal sous le regard sidéré des passants.

Une foule qui a bien vu un homme remonter à la surface, avant l'arrivée de la propriétaire, mais ce dernier ne sortait pas du véhicule. Il s'agissait d'un sauveteur qui s'était immédiatement jeté dans le port au cas où de possibles occupants auraient besoin d'aide.

De retour sur terre à la nage, c'est donc également lui qui a été réchauffé par les sapeurs-pompiers avant que les gendarmes ne recueillent son témoignage.

Choisissez la bonne réponse, A, B ou C.

1 Qu'est-ce qui s'est passé, jeudi dernier à Port-Vendres?
   A ☐ Une voiture est tombée dans l'eau.
   B ☐ Une voiture a percuté une autre voiture.
   C ☐ Une voiture a renversé un cycliste.

2 Pourquoi l'accident s'est-t-il produit?
   A ☐ La conductrice a fait une fausse manoeuvre.
   B ☐ La voiture avait glissé sur la chaussée.
   C ☐ La conductrice a agi en étourderie.

3 Qu'est-ce que la conductrice avait oublié?
   A ☐ de faire une course.
   B ☐ d'immobiliser la voiture.
   C ☐ de klaxonner.

4 Qui était l'homme qui est remonté à la surface?
   A ☐ un passager qui sortait de la voiture.
   B ☐ le propriétaire du véhicule.
   C ☐ un sauveteur.

5 Comment l'homme a-t-il regagné le quai?
   A ☐ Sans l'aide de personne.
   B ☐ Les sapeurs-pompiers l'ont aidé.
   C ☐ Il a appelé les gendarmes à son aide.

Task 3
1 a; **2** a; **3** b; **4** c; **5** a

Answers

TAKE A BREAK!

7 On fait des achats

Going shopping

Don't forget to follow the signposts for extra help with learning and memorising at every turning. The Mind Maps on pages 110 – 112 will point you in the right direction when you're in town.

Remember to think positive wherever possible; concentrate on the clothes you like most, or the food you most like to eat.

Once again, try to picture yourself in a French shopping centre with a list of things to do. Could you manage to get everything done?

Help is at hand!

	Notes/Options
1 Où est ...	= Where is ...
la boucherie?	the butcher's?
la boulangerie?	the baker's?
le bureau de tabac?	the tobacconist's?
le centre commercial?	the shopping centre?
la charcuterie?	the delicatessen (pork butcher's)?
la confiserie?	the sweet shop?
l'épicerie?	the grocer's?
la pâtisserie?	the cake shop?
la pharmacie?	the chemist's?
la poissonnerie?	the fishmonger's?
la poste?	the post office?
le supermarché?	the supermarket?

– *Beware!* **La librairie** *is the bookshop* **not** *the library!*

2 A quelle heure ferme le magasin?	= When does the shop close?
Vous fermez à quelle heure?	= When do you close?
Vous ouvrez à quelle heure?	= When do you open?
A quelle heure ouvre le magasin?	= When does the shop open?

At the bank / bureau de change
18 exchange money? check the exchange rate? ask for coins/notes of a certain type?

checklist
What you need to know

In French, can you:	Fine	Help!
Food shopping ...		
1 ask where shops are?	●	●
2 ask for opening times?	●	●
3 ask if they sell ...?	●	●
4 ask for items (by weight, quantity, containers)?	●	●
5 say that it is all you want?	●	●
6 pay for goods and check the change?	●	●
7 understand information about discounts, special offers, and so on?	●	●
Clothes shopping		
8 name the clothes?	●	●
9 give your size?	●	●
10 ask for particular colours and materials?	●	●
11 say you want an item, or why not, and pay?	●	●
12 give simple opinions?	●	●
At the post office		
13 ask where a post office is?	●	●
14 say where you want to send a letter, postcard or parcel? ask how long it will take? ask how much it costs? ask for stamps? ask if there is a telephone nearby?	●	●
15 ask for a phone card?	●	●
16 give your phone number?	●	●
17 ask to make a reverse charge call?	●	●

59

7

HEURES D'OUVERTURE	opening times
lun - ven	= Monday – Friday
de 8h 30 à 12h	de = from à = to
de 14h à 18h 30	14h = 2 pm 18h 30 = 6.30 pm
sam de 8h 30 à 17h 30	sam = Saturday 8.30 am – 5.30 pm

3 Avez-vous ...
   du pain?
   du fromage?
   de l'eau?
   des fraises?

= Do you have ...
   some bread?
   some cheese?
   some water?
   some strawberries?

There are all the necessary items of food within the Mind Map on page 111. Make sure you study it and get a mental picture of it ready for your exam day!

4 Asking for amounts of food

Je voudrais ...			
un demi-kilo	de	raisins	½ kilo
500 grammes de		beurre	500 g
une livre		fraises	a pound
un kilo		bananes	a kilo
un morceau		fromage	a piece of
une portion		frites	a portion of
une tranche		jambon	a slice of
un paquet		thé	a packet of
une bouteille		coca	a bottle of
un litre		lait	a litre of
une douzaine	d'	oeufs	a dozen
une boîte	d'	haricots verts	a tin of

Je suis désolé(e) il n'y a plus de poisson.

= I'm sorry there's no more fish.

5 Et avec ça?

= Is there anything else?

Non, c'est tout.

= No, that's all.

Un peu plus.

= A bit more.

Ça suffit.

= That's enough.

Ça va très bien.

= That's fine.

6 Les bananes sont à combien?

= How much are the bananas?

Le melon coûte combien?

= How much is the melon?

Les bananes sont à 5F le kilo.

= The bananas are 5F a kilo.

Le melon – c'est 8F la pièce.

= The melons are 8F each.

Je vous dois combien?

= How much do I owe you?

Ça fait combien?

C'est combien?

= How much is it?

Ça fait 25F.

J'ai seulement un billet . de 100F

= I've only got a 100F note.

Voici la monnaie.

= Here's the change.

– *Be careful!* **La monnaie** *is change not money*

7 L'argent

= The money

un billet

= a banknote

la pièce

= the coin

la monnaie

= the change

soldes

= sales

en promotion

= on special offer

réduction

= reduction

remise de 5% sur les livres

= 5% off (discount) books

Going for a C?

A

2 derniers jours!
SOLDES
50% sur maillots
de bains

B

Promotion

Fruits de la région

Melons 5F la pièce*

C

Réductions pour les étudiants

Rayon Papeterie Papetene

Circle A, B or C.

1 Where can students get reduced prices on writing materials? A, B or C?

2 Where can you find fruit on special offer? A, B or C?

3 Where can you find half-price swimsuits in the sales? A, B or C?

* Here la pièce = each (not a coin!)

Answers

Going for a C?
1 = C, 2 = B, 3 = A.

8 See the Mind Map on page 111 which is all about the clothes you might want to buy.

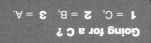

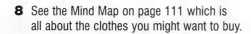

SOLDES
taille 107cm

9 C'est quelle taille?

= What size is it? (used for clothes)

Vous faites quelle pointure?

= What shoe size are you?

Vêtements

30"	=	75 cm	=	soixante-quinze
32"	=	80 cm	=	quatre-vingts
34"	=	86 cm	=	quatre-vingt-six
36"	=	91 cm	=	quatre-vingt-onze
38"	=	97 cm	=	quatre-vingt-dix-sept
40"	=	102 cm	=	cent deux
42"	=	107 cm	=	cent sept
Size 8	=	36	=	trente-six
10	=	38	=	trente-huit
12	=	40	=	quarante
14	=	42	=	quarante-deux
16	=	44	=	quarante-quatre

Chaussures

2	=	35	=	trente-cinq
3	=	36	=	trente-six
4	=	37	=	trente-sept
5	=	38	=	trente-huit
6	=	39	=	trente-neuf
7	=	41	=	quarante et un
8	=	42	=	quarante-deux
9	=	43	=	quarante-trois
10	=	44	=	quarante-quatre

Je fais du 41.	= I'm a size 41.
petit(e)	= small
moyen(ne)	= medium
grand(e)	= large

Revise with the numbers Mind Map on page 120.

10 Revise colours with the Mind Map on page 94.

en coton	= cotton
en soie	= silk
en laine	= wool
en nylon	= nylon
en cuir	= leather
en plastique	= plastic

11

POSITIVE	
J'aime **la** robe.	= I like the dress.
Je **la** prends.	= I'll take it.
C'est à la mode.	= It's fashionable.
C'est cool!	= It's great!
Je préfère …	= I prefer …
J'aime **le** pullover!	= I like the jumper!
Je **le** prends.	= I'll take it.
J'aime **les** chaussures!	= I like the shoes!
Je **les** prends.	= I'll take them.

NEGATIVE	
Je n'aime pas la robe.	= I don't like the dress.
Je ne la prends pas, merci.	= I won't take it, thank you.
C'est démodé.	= It's unfashionable.
C'est trop cher.	= It's too expensive.
Je n'aime pas la couleur.	= I don't like the colour.
Je n'aime pas le pullover.	= I don't like the jumper.
Je ne le prends pas.	= I won't take it.
Je n'aime pas les chaussures.	= I don't like the shoes.
Je ne les prends pas.	= I won't take them.

Vous acceptez les cartes de crédit?	= Do you accept credit cards?

Going for a C?

Work out what is being asked for:

a   Avez-vous un pullover bleu en laine?

b   Je voudrais un pantalon noir en coton?

c   Avez-vous une cravate rouge en soie?

Answers

Going for a C?   **a** blue woollen pullover,
b black cotton trousers   **c** red silk tie

12 Problèmes

Je peux l'essayer?	= Can I try it on?

C'est trop long!   C'est trop court!   C'est trop cher!

C'est trop grand!   C'est trop petit!   Je n'aime pas la couleur!

13 A la poste = At the post office

Où est la poste / le bureau de poste?	= Where is the post office?
Où est la boîte aux lettres?	= Where is the letter box?
pour aller à = où est	– La boîte à lettres *can also be used.*

Bonjour Monsieur c'est combien pour envoyer une lettre en Angleterre s'il vous plaît?

Ça fait trois francs.

Alors un timbre à trois francs s'il vous plaît.

une cabine téléphonique = a phone booth

Il y a un téléphone près d'ici? = Is there a phone nearby?

14 Je voudrais envoyer … = I would like to send …

une lettre = a letter

une carte postale = a postcard

un timbre = a stamp

un paquet = a parcel

peser = to weigh

Ça prendra combien de temps? = How long will it take?

Trois ou quatre jours.

Il fait remplier cette fiche. = You'll have to fill in this form.

15 Je voudrais une carte téléphonique s'il vous plaît. = I'd like a phone card, please.

16 Mon numéro de téléphone c'est le 04-67-58-02-50.

*– Remember – the French give phone numbers as 04, 67, 58, 02, 50 – in tens – zero quatre, **soixante-sept, cinquante-huit, zéro deux, cinquante**. Practise your own phone number in the same way.*

17 Je peux téléphoner en PCV? = Can I make a reverse charge call?

18 Au bureau de change = At the bank

Bonjour Madame, je voudrais changer de l'argent et des chèques de voyage. = I'd like to change some money and some travellers cheques.

Dans quelle devise? = In which currency?
la monnaie = currency, (also means change)

une livre sterling = a pound sterling
Vous avez une pièce d'identité? = Have you got any ID?
Oui, voici mon passeport. = Here's my passport.
Le cours est à combien? = What is the rate of exchange?

C'est à 7 francs 50 la livre. = It's at 7 francs 50 to the pound.

Il y a une commission? = Is there a commission charge?

Je peux avoir des billets de 50 francs et des pièces de 10 francs? = Could I have some 50F notes and some 10F coins?
Signez ici. = Sign here.
Passez à la caisse. = Go to the cash desk.

Merci Madame.

Bonjour Madame. Je voudrais envoyer un paquet en Ecosse s'il vous plaît.

Il faut le peser – voilà ça fait vingt francs Monsieur.

Ça prendra combien de temps?

Trois ou quatre jours. Il fait remplir cette fiche.

Est-ce qu'il y a une cabine téléphonique près d'ici?

Je voudrais un timbre pour l'Angleterre.

publiphone

A la poste

Ça prendra combien de temps / de jours?

Je voudrais envoyer un paquet.

C'est pour envoyer un paquet.

French Revision Guide   **FOUNDATION**

7

Test yourself

Shopping is another very popular examination topic especially in the speaking test and role play exercise. Be ready for an unexpected element signposted by a question mark or an exclamation mark in a box or Répondez à la question on your cue card.

When you are preparing for your role play exercises, think carefully about the situation and try to anticipate the unexpected element which will be a logical step in the situation. Think of all possible elements. Usually the unexpected will be a 'problem' such as there being no more of the item you want to buy so that you have to change your request. Or something might be the wrong size or colour, or too expensive. You might also have to give a simple opinion or preference.

Try to 'spot' the task during your preparation and listen carefully to the examiner. You might need to choose between two items so listen carefully so that you can make the choice and give a reason for your preference.

Here are some more role play exercises.

Task 1

What would you say or ask for each of the items in these pictures?

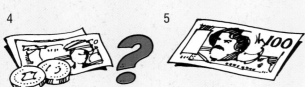

Task 2

A la poste

1 Expliquez.

2 Posez la question.

3 Posez la question.

1 jour...
2 jours...
3 jours...

4 Dites ce que vous voulez.

64

Task 3

Au magasin des chaussures

Examiner: Bonjour Monsieur / Mademoiselle. Vous désirez?

1 Candidate: (Demandez une paire de chaussures. Donnez la couleur.)

Examiner: Bon, des chaussures rouges / noires / bleues, etc. Quelle est votre pointure?

2 Candidate: (Répondez à la question.)

Examiner: Très bien. Voici une paire.

3 Candidate: (Demandez le prix.)

Examiner: Ça fait 300 francs.

4 Candidate: (Vous prenez les chaussures, que dites-vous?)

Examiner: Très bien. Alors passez à la caisse.

Task 4

Listen to the cassette (Side 1, Chapter 7 Foundation). Listen twice.

On fait des achats. Ecoutez les cinq conversations. Ecrivez dans la grille: ce qu'on achète (le produit), la quantité et le prix.

Exemple

Produit	Quantité	Prix
Tomates	1 kilo	4F 90

	Produit	Quantité	Prix
1			
2			
3			
4			
5			

Remember – revise numbers 1–100 (see page 120).

Task 5

A la banque

Vous avez £50 (en billets de banque) et £100 en chèques de voyage.

Imaginez la conversation.
Ecrivez la conversation.

Check back to Notes/Options 18 and see how much you have got right.

Answers

TASK 1
1 Vous avez des bananes?
2 Je voudrais un kilo de bananes.
3 Je voudrais 500 grammes de fraises.
4 C'est combien?
5 J'ai seulement un billet de 100F.

TASK 2
1 Je voudrais envoyer une lettre en Angleterre.
2 Un timbre pour l'Angleterre - ça fait combien?
3 Ça / La lettre prendra combien de temps?
Quand est-ce que la lettre arrivera? = When will the letter arrive?
4 Je voudrais quatre timbres s'il vous plaît.

TASK 3
1 Je voudrais des chaussures rouges / noires / bleues (etc).
2 Je fais du (+ size).
3 C'est combien?
4 Je les prends. Merci.

TASK 4

1	Croissants	3	9F 60
2	Fraises	500g	6F 30
3	Fromage	250g	12F 40
4	Melon	2	13F
5	Champignons	½ kilo	8F 50

On fait des achats

checklist
What you need to know

In French, can you:

	Fine	Help!
1 answer the Foundation Checklist on page 59?	○	○
Clothes shopping		
2 state and explain preferences about clothes / fashion?	○	○
3 make a complaint in a shop, explain the problem and ask for a refund or replacement?	○	○
4 discuss general shopping habits?	○	○
At the post office / making a phone call		
5 explain to somebody how to make a phone call	○	○
6 make a phone call saying who you are and who you wish to speak to?	○	○
7 send a postal order or a telegram?	○	○
8 report the loss of an item (what you've lost, where and when)?	○	○

Going shopping

Don't forget to follow the signposts for extra help with learning and memorising at every turning. The Mind Maps on pages 110 – 12 will point you in the right direction when you're in town.

Remember to think positive wherever possible; concentrate on the clothes you like most, or the food you most like to eat.

Once again, try to picture yourself in a French shopping centre with a list of things to do. Could you manage to get everything done?

Help is at hand!

Notes/Options

1 *Once you've looked back at the Foundation Checklist and you feel confident – carry on!*

2 J'adore le look …

branché = fashionable
décontracté = relaxed
classique = classical

Je préfère porter un jean / un sweat / les vêtements de marque.

un sweat = sweatshirt
les vêtements de marque = branded name clothes

Je n'aime pas porter l'uniforme scolaire.

= I don't like wearing school uniform.

Être à la mode, c'est très important.

= It's important to be fashionable.

Je n'aime pas m'habiller comme tout le monde.

= I don't like dressing like everybody else.

Pour moi, les vêtements sont très importants.

= I think clothes count a lot (are important).

On vous juge selon les vêtements que vous portez.

= People judge you according to what you wear.

3 Problèmes

General
Ça ne marche pas, c'est cassé.

= It doesn't work, it's broken.

Clothes

Il y a une tache.	= There's a stain.
Il manque un bouton.	= There's a button missing.
La fermeture à éclair est cassée.	= The zip is broken.
C'est déchiré.	= It's torn.
Vous pouvez me rembourser?	= Can you give me a refund?
Voici le reçu.	= Here is the receipt.
Pouvez-vous remplacer la robe / le pantalon?	= Can you replace the dress / trousers?
Pouvez-vous faire nettoyer le blouson?	= Can you have the jacket cleaned?
le nettoyage à sec	= dry cleaning

4 Où faites-vous vos provisions?

Be ready in an exam to describe your normal shopping habits (present tense). See the Mind Map on page 123 and page 141. Use a dictionary if you need it.

Je fais mes provisions au supermarché. J'y vais tous les samedis. J'achète de la viande, des légumes et des produits laitiers - et mes produits de ménage - par exemple, la lessive, aux grandes surfaces. Je fais aussi des achats près de chez moi - j'achète mon pain à la boulangerie - au coin de la rue. J'aime faire mes courses au supermarché - je n'ai pas beaucoup de temps et ça m'arrange de faire la plupart de mes provisions une fois par semaine - c'est plus pratique.

J'achète mes vêtements en ville. Je fréquente les grands magasins et les petites boutiques. J'achète, de temps en temps des vêtements de marque mais je trouve que, souvent, ça coûte trop cher! C'est bête de dépenser tellement d'argent sur un ou deux articles! J'adore faire du lèche-vitrines avec mes amis.

faire du lèche-vitrines	= to go window shopping

Remember you must be able to describe a recent shopping trip (perfect tense).

5

un appel téléphonique	= a phone call
décrochez	= pick up the receiver
introduisez une pièce	= put in a coin
attendez la tonalité	= wait for the tone
faites le code	= dial the code
composez le numéro	= dial the number

6

Je voudrais parler à / avec …	= I'd like to speak to …
C'est de la part de James Baker.	= It's James Baker calling.
Je peux lui laisser un message?	= Can I leave him / her a message?

When answering the phone in France, people say Allô and don't tend to give the number as you would in England.

7

Je voudrais envoyer un mandat-postal / un télégramme en Angleterre.	un mandat postal = a postal order un télégramme = a telegram

8

Au bureau des objets trouvés	= At the lost property office

J'ai perdu mon appareil.
　　　　　ma montre.
　　　　　mon sac.

Quand?
C'était hier.
　　　 ce matin.
　　　 il y a deux heures
　　　 (two hours ago).

Où?
Je l'ai perdu(e) dans le parc.
　　　　　　　 dans le bus.
　　　　　　　 en ville.

Décrivez l'objet.
C'est (+ couleur)
C'est en coton / en laine / en cuir / en métal / en argent (silver) / en or (gold).

C'est marqué à mon nom (my name is on it).

C'est de quelle marque?　　= What make is it?
C'est un appareil Canon.
　　 une montre Swatch.

Going for an A?

There is a lot of scope at this level to allow you to give your personal opinions and the reasons for your opinions. You should, however, not only be able to give facts and personal opinions, but also understand the opinions of others.

Learn the expressions Notes/Options 2 and all the new vocabulary.

Remember that most of the exam listening and reading questions will be in French, but there will be at least one exercise which will require answers in English. Remember, if the questions are in English answer in English.

When you are revising, and in the exam use a dictionary to help you with new words, but try to answer as many of the questions as you can before you look things up.

Test yourself

Task 1

Read these letters sent in to a magazine. Answer Questions 1 – 4 in English and tick the correct box for number 5.

Je trouve que porter des vêtements de marque c'est nul. Ce n'est pas parce qu'on porte des trucs de marque qu'on se fait plus d'amis. Je n'ai rien de marque mais, en revanche j'ai plein d'amis - ils me trouvent sympa. Ce qui les intéresse, c'est mon caractère et non mes habits alors … sois naturelle et sympa avec tout le monde, c'est ça le secret pour bien être.

Charlotte, 15 ans, Perpignon

Bien sûr, il faut porter des vêtements de marque! Cela nous permet d'adopter un style, de montrer notre personnalité et de nous affirmer.

Les habits sans marque sont communs, et ceux qui les portent prouvent leur manque de goût. Mais chacun peut penser ce qu'il veut et certains de mes amis s'habillent sans marques.

Marie-Cécile, 16 ans, Besançon

1 According to Charlotte what can designer clothes not help you do?

2 Why does Charlotte think she has a lot of friends?

3 Why does Marie-Cécile think designer clothes are important (give two details).

4 What does she think about people who don't wear designer clothes?

5 Marie-Cécile's last comment shows that:
   a all her friends wear designer clothes. ☐
   b all of her friends wear non-designer clothes. ☐
   c she does not notice what her friends wear. ☐
   d some of her friends wear designer clothes. ☐

TAKE A BREAK!

Now look back at the Checklist on page 66 – you should now be feeling fine for all of the questions.

8

Au café / Au restaurant

Going for a snack?

The Mind Maps on pages 113 – 14 should give you plenty of ideas about what you need to know about this topic area. Everyone loves food in one way or another! Enjoy talking about your likes and dislikes! At this stage, you might like to draw your own Mind Map of, for example, your ideal meal, a healthy meal or an unhealthy one!

Help is at hand!

Notes/Options

1 Tu aimes le fromage?

Oui, j'aime le fromage.
j'aime beaucoup le fromage.
j'adore le fromage.

= I like cheese.
= I really like (like very much) cheese.
= I love cheese.

Mon plat préféré c'est …

= My favourite dish is …

C'est très bon!
C'était très bon!

It's good!
It was good!
– *Always use* **bon** *for good when describing food or drink.*

C'est délicieux!
C'était délicieux!

Tu aimes le poisson?

Je n'aime pas le poisson.
Je déteste le poisson

Ce n'est pas bon!

Je ne mange pas de poisson.

= I don't eat fish.

Ça me rend malade!

= It makes me feel ill!

checklist
What you need to know

In French, can you:

		Fine	Help!
1	express simple opinions about food?	⬤	⬤
2	accept / decline offers of food and drink?	⬤	⬤
3	ask for a table for yourself / a group of people?	⬤	⬤
4	say you have reserved a table?	⬤	⬤
5	attract the waiter's / waitress' attention?	⬤	⬤
6	ask for food and items on the table?	⬤	⬤
7	ask about availability of food and drink?	⬤	⬤
8	ask for the menu?	⬤	⬤
9	ask for a fixed price menu?	⬤	⬤
10	choose and order drinks, snacks, meals?	⬤	⬤
11	ask for an explanation of something on the menu?	⬤	⬤
12	ask for things missing from the table?	⬤	⬤
13	make a simple complaint?	⬤	⬤
14	express simple opinions about a meal?	⬤	⬤
15	ask for and settle the bill?	⬤	⬤

8

2 Tu veux / Vous voulez du pain? = Do you want some bread?

Oui, je veux bien s'il te / vous plaît. = Yes please, I'd like some.

Tu veux / Vous voulez encore du pain? = Do you want some more bread?

Oui, je veux bien.
Oui, je voudrais encore du pain. = Yes, I'd like some more bread.

Je peux reprendre de la glace? = Can I have some more ice-cream?

Oui, bien sûr, sers-toi / servez-vous! = Yes of course, help yourself.

Tu veux / Vous voulez (encore) de la viande? = Do you want some (more) meat?

Oui, s'il te plaît / s'il vous plaît, j'ai faim! = Yes please, I'm hungry!

Merci – j'ai assez mangé. = No thank you – I've eaten enough.
– Remember merci *can mean* no *as well as* thank you.
assez = enough.

Tu veux / Vous voulez encore de l'eau?

Merci, j'ai assez bu. = I've had enough to drink.

3 Je voudrais une table pour trois personnes.

4 J'ai réservé une table. = I've reserved a table.

C'est au nom de Woods. = It's in the name of Woods.
– Be prepared to spell your name!

5 Garçon! = Waiter!

S'il vous plaît Monsieur = to the waiter
           Madame = to the waitress
           Mademoiselle = to a young waitress (of your age)

6 Tu peux / Vous pouvez me passer le beurre s'il te plaît / s'il vous plaît? = Please would you pass me the butter?

– Remember vous *is used to address older people and/or people you do not know well.*

Tu me passes le sel s'il te plaît? le sel = the salt

Vous me passez le poivre s'il vous plaît? le poivre = the pepper

7 Vous avez du poisson? = Have you any fish?

Vous avez des frites? = Have you any chips?

Vous avez des sandwichs au jambon? = Have you any ham sandwiches?

8 Je peux avoir la carte s'il vous plaît? la carte = the menu

Je voudrais la carte des vins s'il vous plaît? la carte des vins = the wine list

9 Je voudrais le menu à 75 francs. = I'd like the 75 francs menu.

10 Qu'est-ce que vous prenez? = What are you having?

Je voudrais commander. = I'd like to order.

Je prends … = I'll have …

Je voudrais … = I'd like …

Comme entrée, je prends le pâté
et comme plat principal, je prends le poulet. = I'll have the pâté to start with.
= as a main course
= I'll have the chicken.

Et pour mon père, le poisson. pour mon père = for my father

Et vous désirez des légumes? légumes = vegetables

Oui, je voudrais des haricots verts et
mon père voudrait des pommes vapeur. = my father would like boiled potatoes

Vous voulez un dessert? dessert = dessert / sweet

Oui, comme dessert … une tarte aux pommes et une glace.

Qu'est-ce que vous prenez comme boissons? = What would you like to drink?
une boisson = a drink

Du vin, une bouteille de vin rouge.

Remember the Mind Maps on pages 113 – 14 to revise snacks, drinks and meals.

11 Le coq au vin, qu'est que c'est? = What is 'coq au vin'?

C'est du poulet cuisiné dans une sauce avec du vin et des champignons – c'est bon!
cuisiné = cooked
préparé avec = prepared with

12 Something's missing!

Garçon, il manque une fourchette! = Waiter, there's a fork missing!
un couteau = a knife
une cuillère = a spoon

Je n'ai pas de couteau. = I haven't got a knife.

Il n'y a pas de sel / de poivre / de sucre. = There isn't any salt / pepper / sugar.

Je voudrais de la moutarde. = I'd like some mustard please.

13 Something's wrong!

Le potage est froid. = The soup is cold.

Le steak n'est pas assez cuit. = The steak isn't cooked enough.

cuit = cooked

Le poisson est trop cuit. = The fish is too well done.

J'ai commandé un steak à point / saignant.
à point = medium
saignant = rare

J'ai commandé mon repas il y a 40 minutes. = I ordered my meal 40 minutes ago.

J'attends depuis une heure! = I've been waiting for an hour!

14 Vous avez bien mangé? = Have you eaten well? / How was your meal?

C'était très bon / délicieux. = It was very good / delicious.

On a bien mangé! = We've eaten well.

J'ai bien mangé - merci! = I've eaten well – thank you!

15 L'addition s'il vous plaît. = The bill please.

Je voudrais l'addition / payer. = I'd like the bill / to pay.

Le service est compris? = Is the service included?

Les boissons sont comprises? = Are the drinks included?

boissons en sus = drinks extra
(often seen written on a menu)

Vous acceptez les cartes de crédit? = Do you accept credit cards?

Il y a une erreur dans l'addition? = There's a mistake in the bill.

Je n'ai pas pris le poisson. = I didn't have the fish.

Going for a C?

Learn all the vocabulary on pages 113 – 14.

Be prepared to talk about your likes and dislikes.

Give simple opinions about your favourite food.

- Remember talking about food can come up in other topics such as holidays – be ready to talk about the kind of food you ate in a different country. The French love to hear foreigners congratulating them on their cuisine.

En France j'ai mangé / j'ai pris …

J'ai adoré la cuisine française! = I loved French cooking!

Test yourself

Try these role play exercises.

You are ordering a snack and drinks for yourself and a friend in a café.

1  Dites ce que vous voulez.

2  Dites ce que vous voulez.

3  Posez la question.

4  Dites ce que vous voulez.

5   Posez la question.

Task 2

Au restaurant

> Bonsoir, je peux vous aider?

1

Dites ce que vous voulez.

> Où voulez-vous asseoir?

2 Répondez à la question.

> Très bien. Voici le menu.
> Que désirez-vous comme entrée?

3 Commandez deux entrées.

> Bon. Et comme plat principal?

4

Posez la question et commandez un plat principal.

> Oui, le poisson est très bon.

5

Posez la question.

Task 3

Des problèmes au restaurant!

1

2

3

4

Dites ce que vous voulez.

Expliquez le problème.

Expliquez le problème.

Dites ce que vous voulez.

Task 4

Lisez ce menu.

RESTAURANT CENTRAL	
Les Entrées	
Potage de légumes	22F
Pâté maison	18F
Melon	17F
Les Plats	
Steak grillé	64F
Truite meunière	49F
Coq au vin	47F
Côtelettes de porc	54F
(sauce à la crème)	
Omelette aux fines herbes	32F
Les Légumes	
Pommes vapeur	10F
Haricots verts	17F
Petits pois	15F
Les Desserts	
Plateau de fromages	17F
Crème caramel	16F
Glace (vanille/fraise)	18F
Tarte aux pommes	21F
Les Boissons	
Vin rouge:	
Vin de pays de Murviel	28F
Vin blanc:	
Château Cayan AOC	34F
Jus de fruits	11F
Eau minérale (Badoit)	16F
Servis compris	

C'est combien?

Exemple

= .... F

1  = ... F

2  = ... F

3  = ... F

4  = ... F

5  = ... F

6 = ... F

7 = ... F

Task 5

Au restaurant

Listen to the cassette (Side 1, Chapter 8
Foundation). Play it twice.

Choisissez deux lettres pour chaque personne.

Exemple =   [B] + [E]

1 ☐ + ☐

2 ☐ + ☐

3 ☐ + ☐

4 ☐ + ☐

A

B

C

D

E

F

G

H

I

J

K

L

M

N

8

Au café / Au restaurant

Going for a snack?

The Mind Maps on pages 113 – 14 should give you plenty of ideas about what you need to know about this topic area. Everyone loves food in one way or another! Enjoy talking about your likes and dislikes! At this stage, you might like to draw your own Mind Map of, for example, your ideal meal, a healthy meal or an unhealthy one!

Help is at hand!

Notes/Options

1 *Once you've looked back at the Foundation Checklist and you feel confident – carry on!*

2 (See also Chapter 2 Higher Checklist 2 – page 22)

Vous voulez encore du poisson?

Je veux bien, c'est délicieux, j'ai très faim.

Ça sent bon!	= It smells good!

Tu veux encore de la pizza?
Merci, je ne l'aime pas trop – c'est un peu trop salé – je n'aime pas trop le goût.

= No thank you – I don't like it very much – it's too salty. I don't like the taste very much.

Tu veux encore de la tarte?
Oui, je veux

un peu	= a bit
un peu plus	= a bit more
la moitié { de la tranche	= half of the slice
{ de la portion	= half of the portion
Ça suffit!	= That's enough!
J'en ai assez merci.	= I've got enough thank you.

3 Vous êtes combien?

Nous sommes cinq.	= There are five of us.
On est cinq.	= There are five of us.

checklist
What you need to know

In French, can you:

		Fine	Help!
1	answer the Foundation Checklist questions on page 69?		

If you've ticked the Help! box, go back to the Foundation Notes/Options and revise.

		Fine	Help!
2	react to offers of food and drink and give your reasons?		
	say how much more you want?		
3	say how many there are in a group?		
4	say where exactly you want to sit?		
5	order a meal and change your order if something is not available?		
6	make a complaint about a meal / the service?		

8

4 Où voulez-vous vous asseoir?

On voudrait s'asseoir près de la fenêtre.	= We'd like to sit near the window.
une table à la terrasse	= a table on the terrace
à l'intérieur	= inside

5

Que prenez-vous comme entrée Monsieur?

Je voudrais les hors-d'oeuvre s'il vous plaît.

Et comme plat principal?

Qu'est-ce que vous recommandez?

Le veau est très bon ce soir.

Bon alors le veau s'il vous plaît.

Qu'est ce que vous recommandez?	= What do you recommend?
Il n'y a plus de veau!	= there's no more veal!
le plat du jour	= the dish of the day

Je regrette Monsieur il n y a plus de veau.

Ah non – alors quel est le plat du jour?

Bon alors – je prends le gigot.

Le plat du jour c'est le gigot – c'est délicieux!

Merci Monsieur.

6 Encore des problèmes!

– See also Foundation Checklist 13, page 71.

Je n'ai pas commandé le poulet!	= I didn't order the chicken!
J'ai commandé il y a 30 minutes.	= I ordered 30 minutes ago.
J'attends depuis une heure!	= I've been waiting for an hour!
Mon verre couteau assiette Ma fourchette } est sale.	= My glass knife plate fork } is dirty.
On peut avoir du sel / du sucre?	= May we have some salt / sugar?
Voulez-vous changer l'assiette?	= Please change the plate.

Going for an A?

Remember to revise preferences about food and drink . You should also be able to understand the opinions of other people about food and drink.

Be prepared to talk about a recent trip you have made to a restaurant in France, elsewhere abroad or in the UK.

Food and drink, likes and dislikes could come up in conversations which include Daily Routine and Health and Fitness (attitudes to heathy and unhealthy eating habits) (see Chapters 1 and 2).

Test yourself

Task 1

> **Restaurant de la Place**
> **Fêtez votre anniversaire!**
> **Menu spécial - 95F**
> **(Gâteau compris!)**

You have decided to celebrate your sister's 18th birthday. You telephone this restaurant to reserve a table.

Allô, Restaurant de la Place, je peux vous aider.

1 Expliquez ce que vous voulez faire.

Alors, c'est pour quand?

2 Dites pour quand vous voulez la réservation (date + heure).

C'est pour combien de personnes?

3 Répondez à la question.

C'est pour une fête spéciale?

4 Éxpliquez ce que vous fêtez.

Bon on va préparer un gâteau – comment s'appelle votre soeur?

Comment s'écrit son prénom?

5 Épelez le prénom de votre soeur (pour le gâteau!).

Task 2

Last year you stayed at Eliane's house. While you were there she celebrated her birthday. Recount what you did on her birthday.

Se lever de bonne heure
Dire 'bon anniversaire'
Donner un cadeau à Eliane
Sa réaction?

Téléphoner au restaurant - pourquoi?
Inviter des copains

Se préparer
Se doucher et s'habiller
Sortir - à quelle heure?
Aller au restaurant

Entrer dans le restaurant
Beaucoup de monde
Commander le repas
Boire un apéritif

Qu'avez-vous mangé et bu?
C'était bon?
Des problèmes?
Demander à voir le patron.

Le patron - s'excuser
Offrir un gâteau à Eliane
Boire du champagne
Payer l'addition
Rentrer - comment?

– Try to give a clear progression through the events in past tenses.

– Add in extra detail if you can. Use **nous** (or **on**) to describe what the group did as well as what you did (**je**).

– *Check that all the verbs in the perfect tense are correct (see pages 122 and 141).*

Now listen to a version of the account on the cassette Side 1, Chapter 8 Higher.

Now have a go at writing out your account. Start off with:

"L'année dernière j'ai fêté l'anniversaire de mon amie Eliane. J'étais en vacances chez elle …"

Task 3

Remplissez les blancs dans cette lettre.

Chère Juliette,

Salut! Merci de ton (1)_____ d'anniversaire. Ça m'a fait plaisir - c'était chouette. J'ai (2)_____ mon anniversaire avec mes copains, Marc, Anne et Olivier. On est (3)_____ au restaurant italien - tu sais que j'adore la (4)_____ italienne. Marc a dit qu'il avait (5)_____ une table mais en arrivant il a (6)_____ qu'il n'y avait pas de réservation! On a dû (7)_____ une heure avant de manger - on avait (8)_____ ! Finalement à 10 heures on a (9)_____ des pâtes mais le serveur a apporté des pizzas! Quel restaurant. On a bien rigolé - heureusement. En plus le serveur qui ne parlait pas un mot de français s'est trompé et l'(10)_____ n'était pas correcte- c'était trop cher. Marc s'est mis en colère mais nous, on a bien rigolé. L'année prochaine je crois qu'on ira dans un restaurant français!

Answers

TASK 1
1 Je voudrais faire une réservation.
2 C'est pour (date + heure).
3 C'est pour (numéro) personnes.
4 On va fêter les 18 ans / l'anniversaire de ma soeur.
5 Ça s'écrit M-A-R-I-A

TASK 3
1 cadeau **2** fêté **3** allé/s **4** cuisine **5** réservé
6 vu/trouvé/découvert **7** attendre **8** faim
9 commandé **10** addition

Au collège

checklist
What you need to know

In French, can you:

		Fine	Help!
1	give details about your school (size, type, buildings, facilities, number of pupils)?	◯	◯
2	ask for and give details about your school routine (timetable, class, homework, games)?	◯	◯
3	give a simple description of your school uniform?	◯	◯
4	say how you travel to and from school?	◯	◯
5	say which subjects you like / dislike and give simple reasons?	◯	◯
6	say which school clubs / teams you belong to?	◯	◯
7	give simple opinions about your school life?	◯	◯
8	say if you intend to leave or stay on at school?	◯	◯

9

Busy at school

The two Mind Maps on pages 115 – 16 are all about school and what you do there, as well as the subjects that you learn. Learn the vocabulary and try to draw your own Mind Maps; for example draw one to represent your own timetable of subjects, or your favourite class.

Help is at hand!

Notes/Options

1 Tu vas à quelle école?
Mon collège s'appelle (+ name)   11–16 school
Mon lycée s'appelle (+ name)   11–18 school

Comment est ton collège?
C'est un collège mixte.
C'est petit / grand.
un collège pour les garçons
un collège pour les filles
un collège catholique

Comment sont les bâtiments?
les bâtiments   = the buildings

Ils sont vieux / modernes.   = They are old / modern.

Il y a des préfabriqués.   = There are mobile classrooms.

Il y a des laboratoires = laboratories
un laboratoire de langues = a language laboratory

une salle d'informatique = IT room
des terrains de sport = sports pitches
une bibliothèque = a library
un gymnase = a gymnasium
un complexe sportif = a sports centre / block

des courts de tennis = tennis courts
une cour = a courtyard
une cantine = a dining room

– Be careful: **un cours = *a lesson!***

Il y a combien d'élèves?
Il y a mille élèves. = There are 1000 pupils.

Il y en a mille. = There are 1000 (of them).

Il y a six cent cinquante élèves. = There are 650 pupils.

2 Tu es en quelle classe?
Je suis en seconde. en seconde = Year II

Comment est ton emploi du temps? = What's your timetable like?

une matière = a school subject
Tu as quelles matières le lundi?
Le lundi j'ai (de l') anglais de 9h à 10h. = from 9 to 10 o'clock
      (du) français.
      (des) sciences.

The Mind Map on page 116 will help you to revise all the school subjects.

A quelle heure commencent les cours? = What time do lessons start?
Les cours commencent à neuf heures.

A quelle heure finissent les cours? = When do lessons finish?
Les cours finissent à quatre heures.

Combien de temps dure un cours? = How long does a lesson last?

Un cours dure 40 minutes / une heure. = A lesson lasts 40 minutes / one hour.

La récréation est à quelle heure? la récréation = break
La récréation est à 11 heures.

Que fais-tu pendant la récréation?
Je joue aux cartes, je prends un casse-croûte et je bavarde avec mes amis. un casse-croûte = a snack
je bavarde = I chat

A quelle heure prends-tu le déjeuner?
Je prends le déjeuner à une heure à la cantine.

As-tu beaucoup de devoirs?
J'ai deux heures par / chaque soir. = I have two hours per / each evening.

Oui, j'en ai trop! = Yes, I have too much!

Tu fais du sport au collège?
Oui, je joue au football, au tennis et je fais de la gymnastique.

See page 100 for all the other sports vocabulary.

3 Tu portes un uniforme scolaire?

Oui je porte un pullover ___?___ *Fill in the colours*
un pantalon ___?___ / une jupe *that you wear!*
___?___ et une chemise ___?___ .

You can revise clothes vocabulary again by looking at the Mind Map on page 111, and for the colours look at page 94.

4 Comment viens-tu à l'école / au collège? = How do you come to school?

Je viens à pied / à vélo / en voiture / en car. en car = by bus / coach

5 Quelle matière préfères-tu?
Pourquoi?

POSITIVE	
Je préfère	l'anglais
J'adore	le français
J'aime beaucoup	les maths
	la biologie
	la géographie
C'est intéressant	= interesting
C'est facile	= easy
C'est utile	= useful
C'est amusant	= funny
Je suis fort(e) en géo	= I'm good at geography
J'aime le prof!	= I like the teacher!

Quelle matière est-ce que tu n'aimes pas? Pourquoi pas?

NEGATIVE	
Je déteste	le sport
Je n'aime pas du tout	la technologie
	l'allemand
	les sciences
C'est ennuyeux	= boring
C'est dur	= hard
C'est difficile	= difficult
Je suis faible en maths.	= I'm poor at maths.
Je n'aime pas le prof!	= I don't like the teacher.

6 Tu fais partie / d'un club / d'une équipe scolaire? = Do you belong to a school club / team?

Oui, je fais partie du …. = Yes, I'm a member of the …

club de drame = drama club
club d'échecs = chess club
club de photo = photo club

Oui je fais partie de l'équipe
  de rugby
  de tennis
  de netball

I'm a member of the … team

7 Que penses-tu de ton collège?

POSITIVE	
Je l'aime!	J'ai beaucoup d'amis au collège.
	Les classes sont intéressantes.
	C'est un bon collège.
NEGATIVE	
Je ne l'aime pas!	Je n'ai pas beaucoup d'amis.
	C'est ennuyeux.
	C'est trop strict (too strict).

Going for a C?

Add opinions about uniform, and subject, give simple reasons why.

Talk about what you did yesterday at school – use the following help.

Hier	
j'ai fait	= I did / had
j'ai pris	= I took
j'ai travaillé	= I worked
j'ai mangé	= I ate
les classes ont commencé à	= lessons started at
je suis venu(e) au collège	= I came to school

Record Checklist questions 1 – 8 and leave a space on the cassette for your answer. Try not to look at the book!

8 Qu'est-ce que tu vas faire après les examens?
Tu quitteras l'école?

= What are you going to do after the exams? Will you leave school?

Je resterai à l'école pour passer mes 'A' levels.

= I'll stay at school to take my 'A' levels.

Je quitterai l'école

= I'll leave school.

Ça dépend de mes résultats!

= It depends on my results!

Test yourself

Task 1

Prepare a presentation about your school. Use this Mind Map to help.

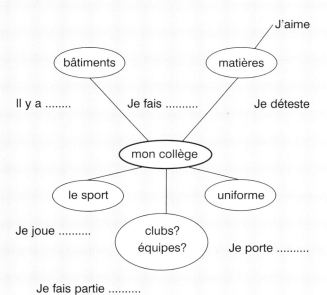

Je fais partie ....

Now record yourself. Play it back and see where you have had difficulty keeping going. Re-do that particular section.

Task 2

Listen to the cassette (Side 1, Chapter 9 Foundation). Play the cassette twice.

Complétez les notes et cochez (✓) la bonne case.

Le collège de Sophie
1 Collège mixte ☐ pour des filles ☐
2 Combien d'élèves? ………………
3 Bâtiments? vieux ☐ modernes ☐
4 Il y a **i** une cantine
   ii ………………
   iii ………………
   iv ………………
5 Sophie préfère ………………
   parce que …………………………………
6 Les classes finissent à ………………h. ….

Task 3

Ecrivez un article (100 mots) au sujet de votre collège.

• Use the Mind Map for the speaking exercise (Task 1) to help!

• Check back to the answers 1 - 8 and correct the French if it is inaccurate.

• Ask a friend who is learning French to read it.

Give yourself a point for each item of information he / she understands. Aim for at least ten points.

• Try to put in your likes / dislikes and give a reason wherever possible.

Answers

TASK 2
1 mixte **2** 700 **3** modernes **4** (i) un gymnase; (ii) des laboratoires; (iii) une bibliothèque **5** le français …, le prof est sympa / amusant **6** 4h 30.

Au collège

checklist
What you need to know

In French, can you:

Fine   Help!

1 do the Foundation Checklist on page 78?

If you've ticked the Help! box, go back and revise.

2 say how long you've been learning French – any other foreign languages you know?

3 talk about your timetable, terms and holidays?

4 discuss school subjects, rules, uniform?

5 say which exams you are taking and discuss your future plans at school?

6 describe special events / trips in the school year?

Busy at school

The two Mind Maps on pages 115 – 16 are all about school and what you do there, as well as the subjects that you learn. Learn the vocabulary and try to draw your own Mind Maps; for example draw one to represent your own timetable of subjects, or your favourite class.

Help is at hand!

Notes/Options

1 *Once you've looked back at the Foundation Checklist and you feel confident – carry on!*

2 Tu apprends le français depuis quand?
J'apprends le français depuis cinq ans.

l'allemand / l'espagnol / l'italien / le russe = German / Spanish / Italian / Russian

3 Tu as combien de semaines de vacances scolaires?
On a } deux semaines à Noël.
J'ai } une semaine pour le mi-trimestre
deux semaines à Pâques
une semaine pour le mi-trimestre
six semaines en été
une semaine pour la Toussaint.
Ça fait 13 semaines en tout.

= half term

= *the half term holiday in October*

C'est assez ou est-ce que tu voudrais des vacances plus longues comme en France?

assez = enough

Non, ça va. En France **on commence plus tôt** le matin et on finit plus tard le soir. En France on a **plus de vacances** mais pendant **le trimestre** scolaire il faut travailler dur et on travaille aussi le samedi matin – **je n'aimerais pas faire ça. Si les vacances sont trop longues on s'ennuie!**

people start earlier

more holidays
the term

I wouldn't like to do that. If the holidays are too long you get bored.

Et comment est ton emploi du temps?

C'est chargé mais assez bien équilibré. Je fais dix matières. Certaines matières sont obligatoires mais on peut aussi choisir certaines matières – il y a des options.

chargé = full / loaded
équilibré = balanced

obligatoire = compulsory
une option = an option

Be prepared to discuss what you do on your favourite / least favourite day, and say why you like / dislike that day.

4 See Foundation Notes/Options 5 and learn the following reasons for liking / disliking subjects / school / uniform.

Use a dictionary to check vocabulary if necessary.

Les matières

POSITIVE ☺ $\frac{18}{20}$	NEGATIVE ☹ $\frac{2}{20}$
Je reçois de bonnes notes.	Je reçois de mauvaises notes.
Je suis fort(e) en maths.	Je suis faible en maths.
Je trouve le travail facile.	Je trouve le travail difficile.
On s'amuse en classe.	On s'ennuie en classe.
Le prof est sympa - il explique bien la matière.	Le prof est nul - il n'explique pas bien la matière.

La discipline

POSITIVE ✔	NEGATIVE ✗
Les profs sont assez stricts mais pas trop.	Les profs ne sont pas assez stricts. Les profs sont trop stricts.
Il y a une bonne ambiance.	Il y a une mauvaise ambiance.
Il n'y a pas trop de bruit.	Il y a trop de bruit.
On peut se concentrer.	On ne peut pas se concentrer.
On s'entend bien avec les profs et les élèves se respectent.	On ne s'entend pas bien avec les profs.
	Les profs et les élèves ne s'entendent pas bien.

L'uniforme

POUR ✔	CONTRE ✗
Le matin, je sais quoi mettre.	Le matin je préfère m'habiller d'une façon différente de mes ami(e)s.
On ne voit pas la différence entre les élèves.	Il faut développer un style personnel.
Porter un uniforme, c'est bien pour la discipline!	
C'est cher au début, mais après, on dépense moins d'argent.	C'est trop cher - acheter un uniforme et d'autres vêtements!
C'est pratique!	Je déteste la couleur - c'est démodé.

5 Tu passes quels examens cet été?

je passe = I'm taking

Je passe des examens, des GCSE en français, en maths …
les examens blancs

= 'mocks' / practice exams

J'espère réussir à mes examens.
rater un examen

= I hope to pass my exams.
= to fail an exam

Si je réussis à mes examens je vais continuer à faire des études.

= If I pass my exams I'm going to carry on with my studies.

Je voudrais passer mes 'A' levels – mon baccalauréat.

le bac = le baccalauréat

Je vais quitter le collège et je voudrais trouver un emploi.

= I'm going to leave school and I'd like to get a job.

6 Pendant l'année scolaire il y a des pièces / des spectacles / des répétitions

plays

= entertainment / rehearsals

des soirées musicales
une journée de compétitions sportives
des réunions pour les parents et les profs
des conseils de classe

= musical evenings
= sports day

= parents' evenings

= staff meetings (to discuss individual class members)

des matchs de foot / tennis

= football / tennis matches

des voyages scolaires
des échanges scolaires
une distribution des prix

= school trips
school exchange trips
Speech Day / Prizegiving

Going for an A?

Be prepared to talk about what **normally** happens at the events in Checklist 6: D'habitude + present tense, on va, on voit, on reçoit, on donne, on regarde.

Be prepared to talk about events last year (perfect + imperfect tenses): L'année dernière, j'ai joué dans une pièce. J'ai joué le rôle de … C'était chouette.

Be prepared to talk about school life in France as well as your own experience.

Remember: plus … que = more than
moins … que = less than

En France la journée scolaire est plus longue mais les vacances sont plus longues.

Test yourself

Task 1

Lisez les paragraphes. Attention! Les trois paragraphes ne sont pas dans le bon ordre!

La vie en terminale – trois moments importants de l'année scolaire

David - élève

A J'ai commencé à réviser en mai – un petit peu tous les jours. Je n'avais pas assez de temps et je ne savais pas trop comment m'y prendre. En juin je m'y suis mis plus sérieusement.

B Dès la rentrée les profs n'ont qu'un mot à la bouche – le bac et encore le bac – ça finit par devenir stressant. On commence la philo – c'est une nouvelle matière – il faut apprendre une méthodologie – c'est dur.

C On a eu un examen blanc – le bac blanc – juste avant les vacances de février. Toutes les matières écrites dans les conditions de l'examen et les vraies copies de l'examen. C'était indispensable car cela m'a permis de voir ce que les profs attendaient de moi. Et on est moins stressé en juin.

Mettez les paragraphes A, B et C dans le bon ordre.

Encerclez la bonne lettre. Exemple (A) B C

Paragraphe **1** = A B C
Paragraphe **2** = A B C
Paragraphe **3** = A B C

Task 2

Lisez les paragraphes suivants.

Mme Panis - professeur

D   S'évaluer c'est l'un des objectifs du bac blanc. Si la surprise est agréable cela vous réconforte – si elle ne l'est pas on a le temps de redresser la barre. Participer à un bac blanc c'est mettre 30% de chances en plus de son côté.

E   Le bac arrive toujours trop vite. Pour éviter d'être débordé au dernier moment mieux vaut s'y prendre le plus tôt possible. L'idéal serait d'avoir terminé vos révisions en juin pour tester vos connaissances à deux ou à l'aide d'exercices.

F   La rentrée, c'est le temps des bonnes résolutions. Elles peuvent se résumer en trois: bien suivre en classe (c'est le début de la mémorisation); reprendre ses notes pour les remettre en ordre; enfin continuer à mener une vie normale – à jouer au basket ou de la guitare si cela vous détend.

Mettez les paragraphes dans le bon ordre.

Paragraphe **1**   =   D   E   F

Paragraphe **2**   =   D   E   F

Paragraphe **3**   =   D   E   F

Task 3

C'est vrai ou c'est faux? Cochez la bonne case. Si c'est faux corrigez l'erreur.

	Vrai	Faux
1 David a commencé beaucoup de nouvelles matières en terminale.	☐	☐
2 David pense que l'examen blanc est une perte de temps.	☐	☐
3 David a commencé à réviser trop tard.	☐	☐
4 Mme Panis conseille aux jeunes de participer à des activités à l'extérieur de l'école.	☐	☐
5 Mme Panis pense qu'il est utile de réviser avec un(e) ami(e).	☐	☐

Task 4

Ecrivez une liste des aspects positifs et négatifs dans votre collège.

POSITIVE	NEGATIVE
Les profs sont sympa. J'ai beaucoup de copains de classe.	Je n'aime pas l'uniforme – c'est démodé.

Use the Notes/Options to help! Try to write at least five positive and five negative things. Say what you would change if you could, eg, si je pouvais changer quelque chose, je ne porterais pas d'uniforme.

You might need to revise the conditional tense again here, so look at page 144.

Make sure you can do the Foundation Speaking task on page 81.

Make a more sophisticated Mind Map which includes Avantages (positive) et Inconvénients (negative). (For help see page 83.)

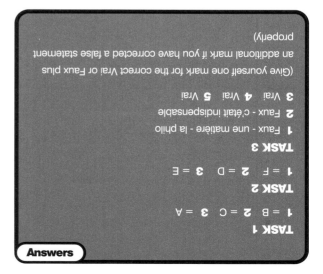

Answers

TASK 1

1 = B   **2** = C   **3** = A

TASK 2

1 = F   **2** = D   **3** = E

TASK 3

1 Faux - une matière - la philo

2 Faux - c'était indispensable

3 Vrai   **4** Vrai   **5** Vrai

(Give yourself one mark for the correct Vrai or Faux plus an additional mark if you have corrected a false statement properly)

checklist
What you need to know

In French, can you:

	Fine	Help!

Work

1 give information about future work plans?

2 give information about how you get to work and how long it takes?

3 say that somebody is out of work?

4 understand details about jobs, weekend jobs and work experiences?

5 say if you have a spare-time job and give details about it (hours, pay)?

6 give simple opinions about jobs?

7 say which jobs you and your family do?

Publicity

8 understand and give simple opinions about adverts?

Communication

9 ask and give a phone number and answer a phone call, saying who you are?

10 ask to speak to someone and take or leave a message?

Back to work

Make sure that you match up the checklist areas where you still need some help with the correct Notes/Options below. By now, you must be familiar with making the most of the Mind Maps. Have a look at page 117. These are particularly useful to give you ideas about what you might do in the future.

Help is at hand!

Notes/Options

1 Qu'est-ce que tu veux faire dans la vie? = What job do you want to do?

Je veux être infirmière. = I want to be a nurse.

J'espère être ingénieur. = I hope to be an engineer.

See the Mind Map on page 117.

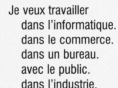

Je veux travailler dans l'informatique.	= I want to work / a job / in computers.
dans le commerce.	= in business.
dans un bureau.	= in an office.
avec le public.	= with the public.
dans l'industrie.	= in industry.
Je veux un métier intéressant.	= I want an interesting job.
un métier	= a job / profession
Je veux continuer avec mes études.	= I want to carry on studying.
Je veux aller / en faculté / à l'université.	= I want to go to university.
Je veux trouver un emploi.	= I want to find a job.
Je veux faire un stage de formation.	= I want to do a training course.
Je veux faire un apprentissage.	= I want to do an apprenticeship.
Je veux faire un stage d'informatique.	= I want to do a computing course.

Je ne sais pus – je n'ai pas encore décidé ...
ça dépend de mes résultats.

= I don't know – I haven't decided yet ...
= it depends on my results.

Think about your future plans. Make sure you can say what you want to do – don't be surprised on the day of the exam!

2 Comment vas-tu au travail?

Je vais en bus / à pied / en train.
Le trajet dure vingt minutes.

= I go by bus / on foot / by train.
The journey takes 20 minutes.

3 Ton père / ta mère / ton frère / ta soeur travaille?

= Does your father / mother / brother / sister work?

Oui il / elle est (+ job).

Non il / elle est au chômage.

au chômage = unemployed

Il est chômeur.

= He is unemployed.

Elle est chômeuse.

= She is unemployed.

4 Les heures de travail sont de 9h à 5h

= The working hours are from 9 – 5 o'clock

un travail à plein temps

= a full time job

un travail à mi-temps

= a part time job

on recherche vendeur

= wanted – a salesman

expérience essentielle

= experience is essential

un bon salaire

= good salary

C'est bien payé.

= It's well paid.

faire un stage

= to do work experience

J'ai fait un stage

= I did my work experience

{ chez (+ name of firm)
  dans un bureau
  dans une usine

{ at (+ firm)
  in an office
  in a factory

J'ai fait un stage de deux semaines.

= I did two weeks' work experience.

un emploi
un boulot (slang)

= un travail
= a job

5 Tu as un travail?
Tu travailles?

= Do you have a job?

Oui je travaille ...
   dans un supermarché
   dans un magasin
   dans un café
   chez (+ name of firm)
   chez un coiffeur

= Yes I work ...
   in a supermarket
   in a shop
   in a café
   at (+ firm)
   at a hairdresser's

Oui je distribue des journaux.
   je fais du babysitting.

= Yes I deliver papers.
   I babysit.

Non je n'ai pas de travail.

= No I haven't got a job.

Je travaille le samedi / tous les soirs / deux soirs par semaine.

I work on Saturdays, every evening / two evenings a week.

C'est bien payé?
Oui, pas mal ...
je reçois } 3 livres de l'heure.
je gagne } 20 livres par jour.

Is it well paid?
Yes it's not bad ...
– I get £3 an hour.
– I earn £20 a day.

Non c'est mal payé/Ce n'est pas bien payé.

= No it's badly paid / It isn't well paid.

Avec l'argent ...
   je fais des achats.
   je fais des économies.

= With the money ...
= I buy things.
= I save up.

Que penses-tu de ton travail?

POSITIVE 😊	NEGATIVE 😧
C'est intéressant.	C'est ennuyeux.
C'est bien payé.	C'est mal payé.
J'aime travailler avec le public.	C'est fatigant.

7 See the Mind Map on page 117.

8 La Publicité: Advertising – useful vocabulary and phrases.

une annonce

= an advert

à mon avis

= in my opinion

la mode

= fashion

une photo

= a photo

une réclame

= an advert

un spot publicitaire

= a TV advert

J'aime la publicité à la télé ... = I like TV advertising
... c'est amusant. = it's funny.

Je déteste la publicité à la
télévision ...
... c'est bête ... = it's stupid
... ça ne représente pas = it doesn't represent
la réalité. reality.

9/10

See Chapter 7 Foundation Checklist 16 –
how to give a phone number.

At home
Allô, **Nicola King** à l'appareil. = Hello (when
answering a call at
home) it's Nicola King
speaking.

At work
Société Smith, Bonjour ... = Smiths, Good
morning ...

See also Chapter 7 Higher Checklist 6 –
leaving a message.

Vous voulez laisser un = Do you want to
message? leave a message?

Oui, c'est de la part de = Yes, it's Chris
Chris Woods. Woods speaking.
Non, je peux rappeler dans = Can I ring back in
une demi-heure? half an hour?

Vous pouvez rappeler ... = You can ring back ...
Ne quittez pas. = Hold on a moment.
Je vous passe à ... = I'm putting you
through to ...

Vous pouvez me donner vos = Can you give me
coordonnées? your details (name and
number)?

Going for a C?

Remember to give opinions about your
choice of job!

Test yourself

Task 1

Try to talk about your job for a minute or
so. Use the following cue card.

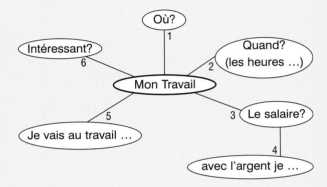

Task 2

Listen to the cassette (Side 1, Chapter 10
Foundation). Play it twice.

Qu'est-ce que vous voulez faire comme travail?

Choisissez un travail – pour chaque personne.

Exemple: Sandrine = C

1 Alain = ☐
2 Anne = ☐
3 David = ☐
4 Sylvie = ☐
5 Nabila = ☐

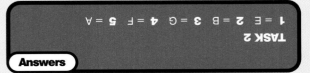

TASK 2
1 = E 2 = B 3 = G 4 = F 5 = A

Answers

10

Back to work

Make sure that you match up the checklist areas where you still need some help with the correct Notes/Options below. By now, you must be familiar with making the most of the Mind Maps. Have a look at page 117. These are particularly useful to give you ideas about what you might do in the future.

Help is at hand!

Notes/Options

1 *Once you've looked back at the Foundation Checklist and you feel confident – carry on!*

2/3 Que voudrais-tu faire dans la vie? Pourquoi?

Je voudrais faire un stage. continuer avec mes études. } parce que/parce qu'

je dois réussir à mes études pour devenir avocat

réussir = to be successful/to pass

aller en faculté   = to go to university.

Il faut faire des études supérieures pour être médecin.
On réussit avec des diplômes.
Les études sont indispensables.

= You have to do further studies to be a doctor.
= You'll succeed with qualifications.
= Studies are essential.

Je voudrais faire un stage, il faut une formation spécialisée pour travailler dans le tourisme.

= You have to have special training to work in tourism.

J'espère devenir professeur.

– *Do not put the 'un' in!*

4 See the Foundation Checklist 4. You should be able to talk and write about the details as well as understand.

Au travail

checklist
What you need to know

In French, can you:

	Fine	Help!
1 do the Foundation Checklist on page 86?		

If you've ticked the Help! box, go back and revise.

	Fine	Help!
2 give reasons for your choice of study or job?		
3 express hopes about your future plans after studying?		
4 give details about jobs, weekend jobs and work experience?		
5 understand and give opinions about different jobs?		
6 make arrangements to be contacted by fax or phone?		
7 ask what work others do?		
8 enquire about the availability of work?		

Going for an A?

Faites correspondre les métiers (1 – 9) aux phrases A – I.   Exemple 1 = D

Métiers	Phrases
– *Je voudrais être / devenir …*	*parce que …*
1 instituteur / institutrice	A je veux aider les gens
2 comptable	B l'actualité m'intéresse
3 informaticien / informaticienne	C je veux travailler en plein air
4 médecin	D j'adore les enfants
5 vétérinaire	E je voudrais travailler à l'étranger et parler des langues
6 journaliste	F les chiffres m'intéressent
7 jardinier / jardinière	G je veux gagner beaucoup d'argent
8 interprète	H l'informatique me passionne
9 président-directeur général (PDG) (managing director)	I je veux soigner les animaux

2 F 3 H 4 A 5 I 6 B 7 C 8 E 9 G

Answers

5 Des opinions sur les métiers – use a dictionary to check vocabulary you are not sure of.

Avantages – POSITIVE	Inconvénients – NEGATIVE
C'est bien payé / rémuneré.	C'est mal payé / rémuneré.
C'est un métier stimulant. intéressant. passionnant.	C'est un métier ennuyeux. sans intérêt.
On peut voir le monde.	C'est fatigant.
On pourrait (= might / would be able to) vivre voyager $\}$ à l'étranger.	On doit travailler dans un bureau.
	Les heures sont longues.
Il y a des possibilités de promotion.	C'est un travail répétitif.
C'est un métier utile – ça rend service au public.	C'est un emploi sans avenir.
	C'est un métier peu assuré (not very secure).

6 Je voudrais envoyer un fax / envoyer un document par fax.

I'd like to send a fax / fax this document.

A l'attention de …

= For the attention of …

Mon numéro de fax est …

= My fax number is …

Vous pouvez me joindre à …

= You can reach / contact me on / at (plus phone number or place).

Mon poste de téléphone est …

= My extension is …

Répondez-moi par fax.

= Fax me a reply.

Laissez un message sur le répondeur.

= Leave a message on the answerphone.

7 Que faites-vous dans la vie?

– used to somebody you do not know well = What's your job?

Quel métier exercez-vous / faites-vous?

= What profession do you practise?

8 Je vous écris pour demander si vous cherchez …
    un vendeur/une vendeuse
    un serveur/une serveuse
    un moniteur/une monitrice
    en été.
s'il y aura un travail temporaire

I'm writing to ask if you need …
= shop assistant
= a waiter / waitress
= an attendant
= in the summer.
= if there will be any temporary work

J'ai lu dans le journal que vous cherchez …

= I read in the paper that you are looking for …

En réponse à votre annonce …

= In reply to your advertisement …

J'aimerais beaucoup travailler …
    en France.
    avec les enfants.
    dans un café.

J'ai déjà travaillé comme …

I've already worked as …

Je suis très intéressé(e) par ce poste.

= This post appeals to me.

Je me permets de vous offrir mes services.

= I should like to apply for this post.

Je suis libre du **5 juillet** au **2 septembre.**

= I'm free from July 5th until September 2nd.

Je vous envoie mon cv.

= I enclose my cv.

Formal signing off:
Espérant que vous prendrez ma demande en considération je vous prie d'agréer, Monsieur / Madame, l'expression de mes sentiments les meilleurs.

Going for an A?

- Be prepared to explain what work experience you have had. Always have a reason why you would be good at this kind of job.

- Be ready to give details about your education, exams, which languages you speak and since when (Chapter 9 Higher Checklist 2).

Test yourself

Task 1

HÔTEL CENTRAL

Recherche serveur/serveuse

juillet – août

anglais indispensable!

Ecrivez une lettre au propriétaire de l'hôtel pour poser votre candidature à ce poste.

"Monsieur,

En réponse à votre annonce, je me permets …"

10

Task 2

You decide to ring up the Central Hotel. You have worked in a hotel as a waiter / waitress and want to work in France this summer. You phone the owner.

Hôtel Central Bonjour.

1 Saluez le / la propriétaire et expliquez pourquoi vous téléphonez.

Ah vous êtes anglais(e)! Depuis quand parlez-vous le français?

2 Répondez à la question.

Et vous avez de l'expérience dans l'hôtellerie?

3 Expliquez **quand** et **où** vous avez travaillé.

Et pourquoi est-ce que ce poste vous intéresse? Quand êtes-vous libre?

4 Expliquez pourquoi vous voulez travailler à l'Hôtel Central. Quand êtes-vous libre?

Bon. Envoyez-moi votre cv et je vais vous rappeler. D'accord?

Task 3

Ecrivez une lettre à une colonie de vacances pour demander s'il y aura du travail temporaire en été.

Remember do not use **Cher** / **Chère** in formal letters.

Remember to sign off properly.

Put in all relevant details about your experience.

Say why you want this job.

Check back to Notes/Options 8.

See the mock exam (Section 3) page 137 for further reading practice related to work.

Answers

TASK 2

Bonjour Monsieur.
Je m'appelle …

1 Je vous téléphone au sujet de l'annonce. J'ai vu que vous demandez un serveur / une serveuse.

2 J'apprends le français depuis cinq ans.

3 Oui, j'ai travaillé comme serveur / serveuse l'année dernière, en été, dans un hôtel en Angleterre.

4 Je voudrais beaucoup travailler en France et j'aime travailler avec le public. Je suis libre du 1er juillet au 31 août.

Merci Monsieur. Au revoir.

TAKE A BREAK!

If you have been working through the chapters in order from 1 to ten – well done! You're nearly finished and ready for your exam. Why not now have a go at the mock exam (Chapter 11)?

Or you could look at the summary on page 93 and see if there are any areas where you still want to build your confidence.

As a recap, why not study the Mind Maps again and make sure you can rely on them for help when you might need it?

For that extra confidence, and those extra marks, have a look at the International World Mind Maps on pages 118 – 19.

Mind Maps

These Mind Maps present vocabulary, phrases and grammar that you need to remember for your GCSE exams. Use the Mind Maps in this book to help you with your revision and make up your own Mind Maps.

In many of the Mind Maps in this book, masculine words are written and underlined in red, while the feminine words are black. This is simply a code. You could use the same, or adopt your own. Likewise the perfect tense is usually written and underlined in blue and the future tense in red (and the present is in black).

If you're short of ideas for the central images to your own Mind Maps, copy some of the ideas in this book. Always use images that you like. Be FLAMBOYANT and EXAGGERATE: it'll help your memory.

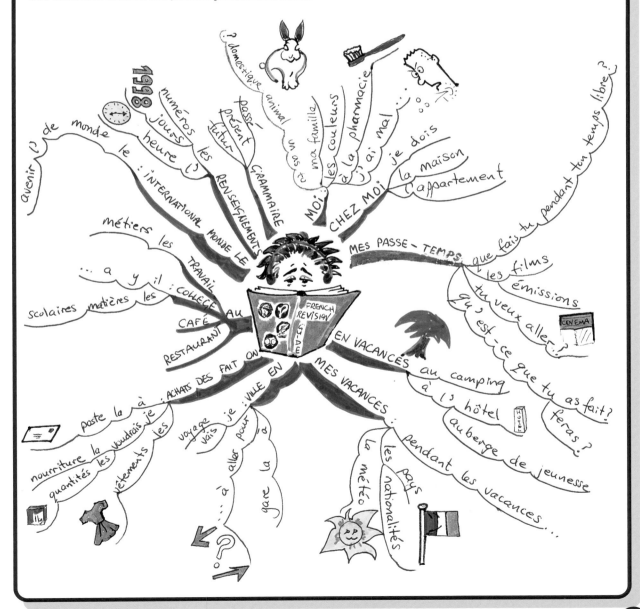

1 Moi

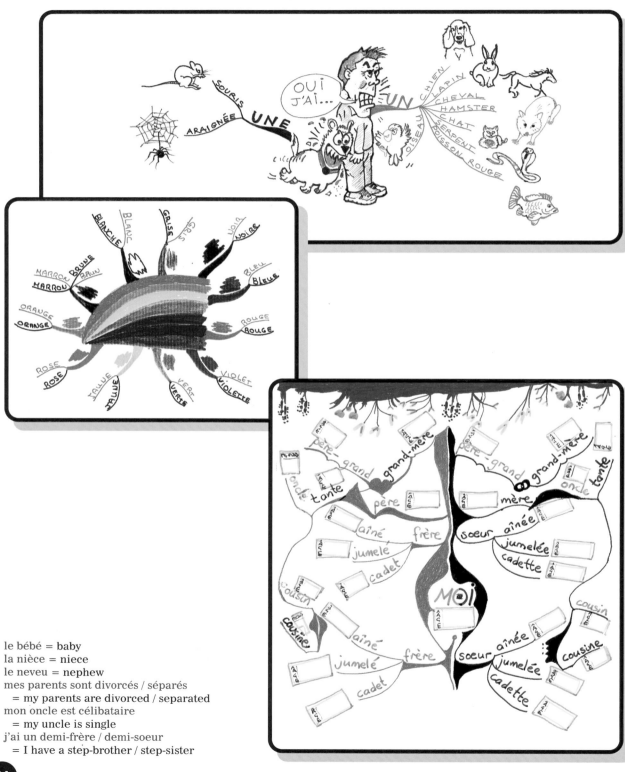

le bébé = baby
la nièce = niece
le neveu = nephew
mes parents sont divorcés / séparés
  = my parents are divorced / separated
mon oncle est célibataire
  = my uncle is single
j'ai un demi-frère / demi-soeur
  = I have a step-brother / step-sister

1 Moi

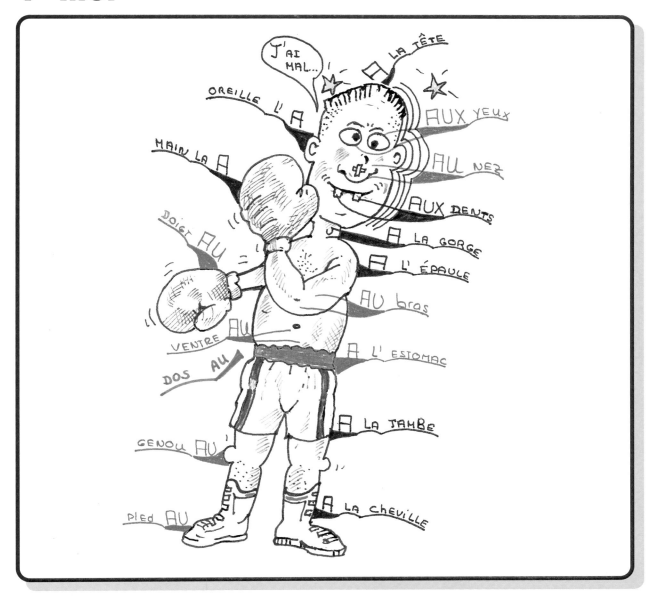

je me suis cassé le bras = I've broken my arm
je me suis coupé le doigt = I've cut my finger
je suis enrhumé(e) = I've got a cold
j'ai la grippe = I've got flu
j'ai de la fièvre = I've got a temperature
j'ai un coup de soleil = I'm sunburnt
je tousse = I'm coughing
je n'ai pas d'appétit = I've lost my appetite
j'ai mal au coeur = I feel sick
je suis malade depuis hier = I've been ill since yesterday
j'ai chaud / froid = I'm hot / cold

1 Moi

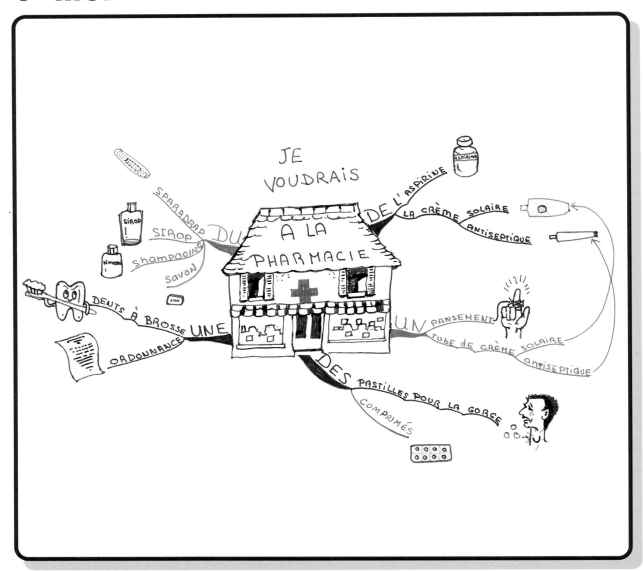

je voudrais un médicament contre les maux de tête = I'd like some medicine for headaches
il faut appeler le médecin = you / one should call the doctor.
quel est le dosage? = what is the dose?
prendre un comprimé le matin et le soir = take one tablet in the morning and in the evening
prendre une cuillerée avant les repas = take one spoonful before meals
nettoyer la plaie = clean the wound
mettre de la crème = apply some cream
rester au lit / garder le lit = stay in bed
ne bougez pas! = don't move!

ez moi

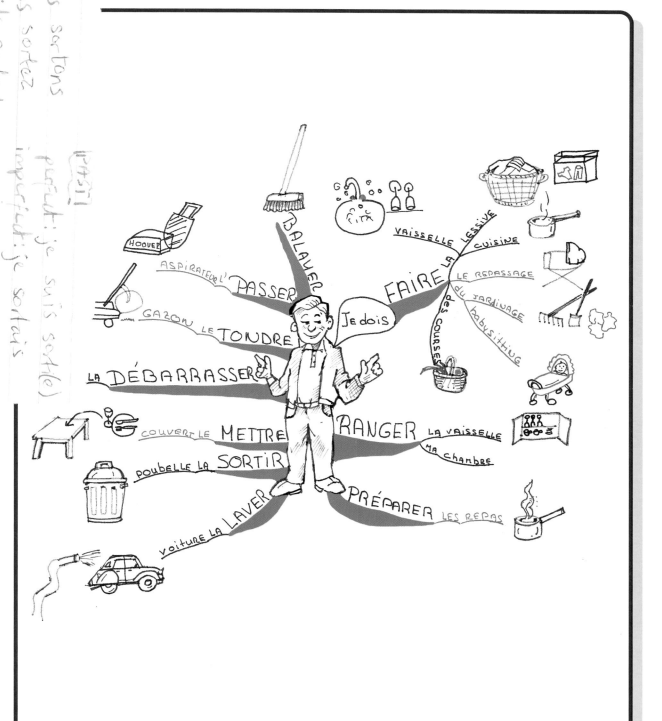

2 Chez moi

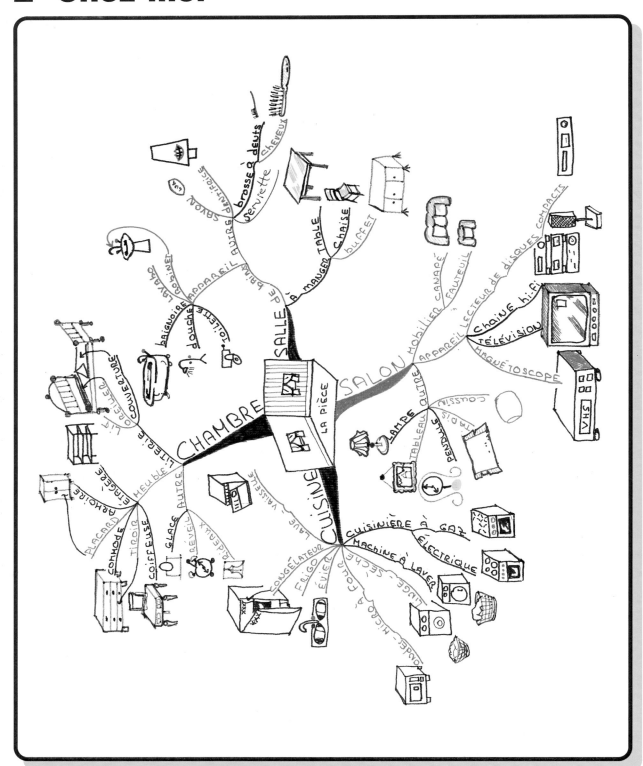

2 Chez moi

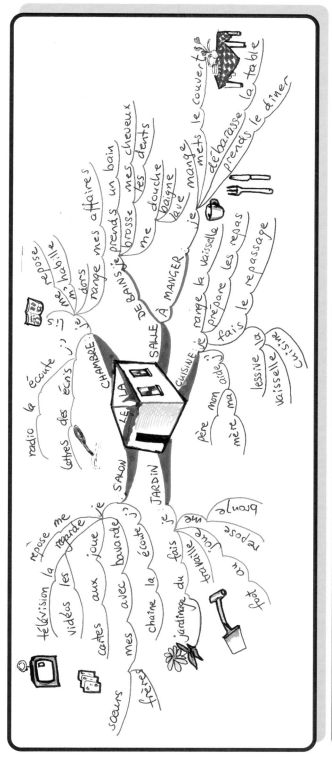

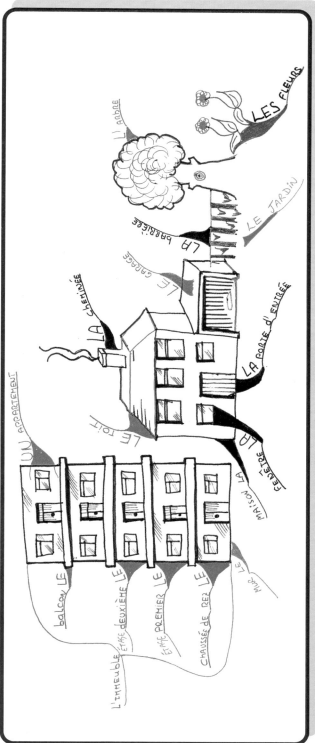

3 Mes passe-temps

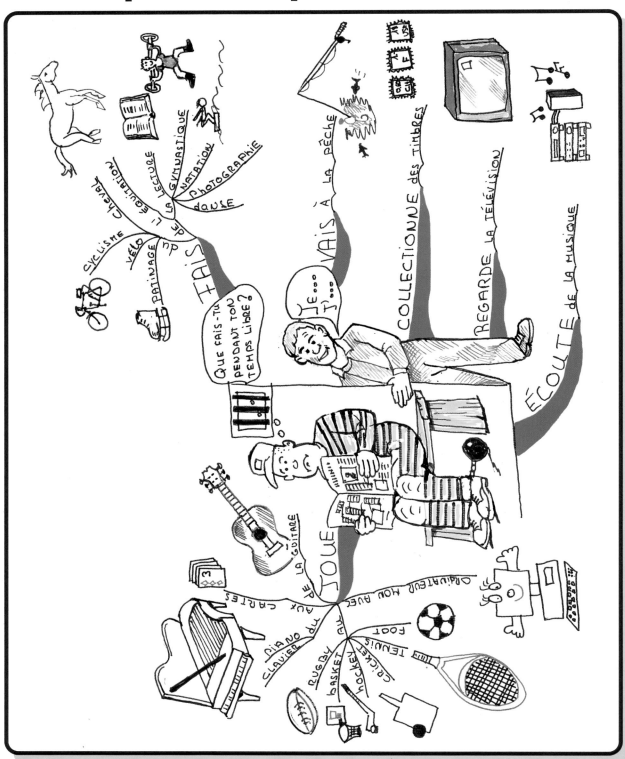

3 Mes passe-temps

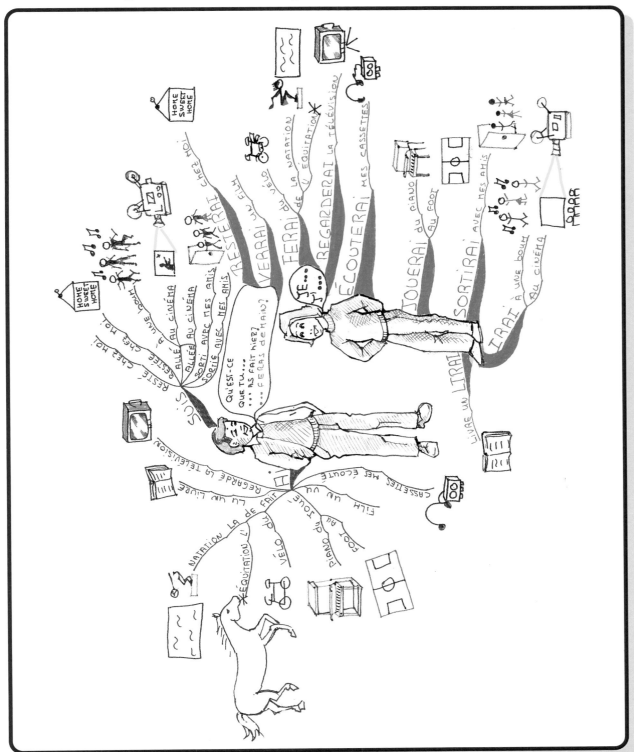

3 Mes passe-temps

j'adore …
il / elle préfère …   } nager
mes parents préfèrent …

j'aime …   } jouer au tennis
mon frère aime …

je déteste …
je n'aime pas …   } lire
mon ami n'aime pas …

C'est chouette   C'est moche

C'était super
 un très bon film
amusant
drôle / marrant
Ça m'a fait rire
Je l'ai trouvé chouette
J'ai adoré le film
Je l'ai beaucoup aimé
L'acteur / L'actrice
joue bien

C'était un mauvais film
 ennuyeux
trop violent
sans imagination
Ça m'a agacé(e) / enervé(e)
Je l'ai trouvé bête
J'ai détesté le film
Je ne l'ai pas aimé
L'acteur / L'actrice ne joue
pas bien

3 Mes passe-temps

danser
gagner
lire
sortir

le basket
le club
le compact disc (CD)
le disque compact (CD)
le disco
le hockey
le jeu = game
le jeu vidéo = video game
le loisir = leisure
le match = match (football)
le membre = member (of a team)
le passe-temps = hobby
le roman = novel / book
le stade = stadium
le terrain (de foot) = (football) pitch

la cassette
la distraction = entertainment
la pêche = fishing
la radio
la surprise-partie = party

l'équipe = team
l'orchestre
l'ordinateur = computer

depuis = since
souvent = often
une fois = once

acheter
commencer
couter
fermer
ouvrir
réserver
trouver

le bal = ball / dance
le balcon = balcony
le férié = public holiday
le programme
le spectacle = show
le ticket

la brochure
la personne
la place = seat

la réduction = reduction
la salle = auditorium
la séance = performance

l'après-midi
l'entrée = l'admission / entry fee

à partir de = from (in time)
jusqu'à = until
toujours = always

cher = expensive
interdit = forbidden
réduit = reduced
sauf = except
sportif = sporty (person)

4 En vacances

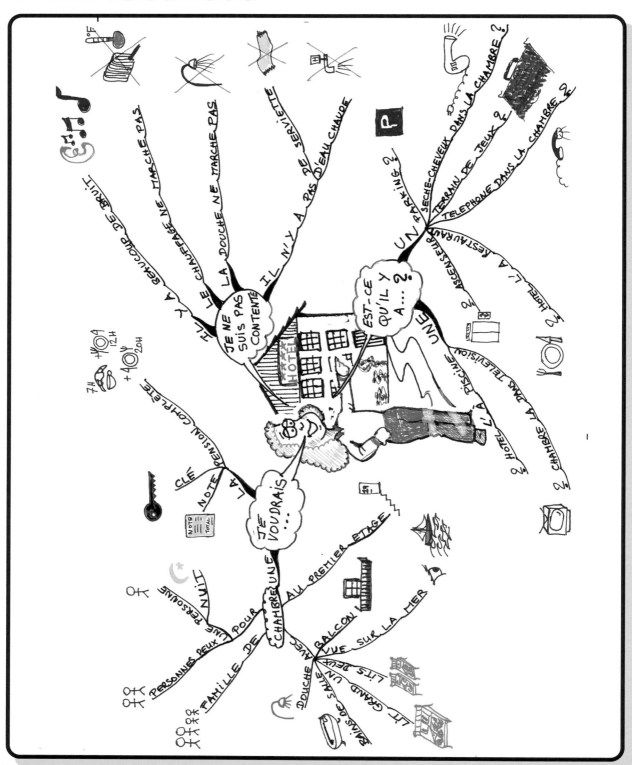

4 En vacances

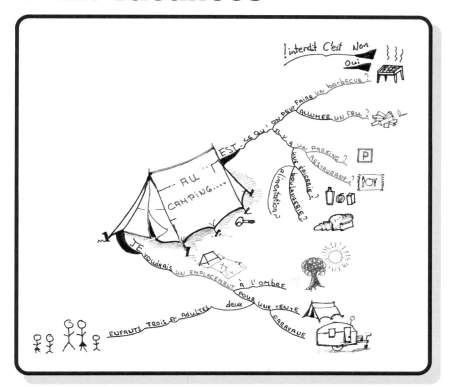

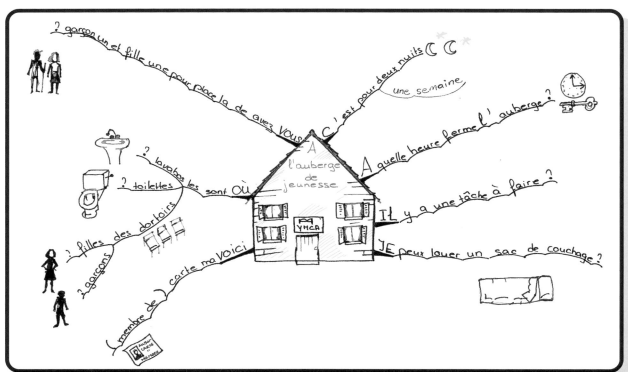

5 Mes vacances

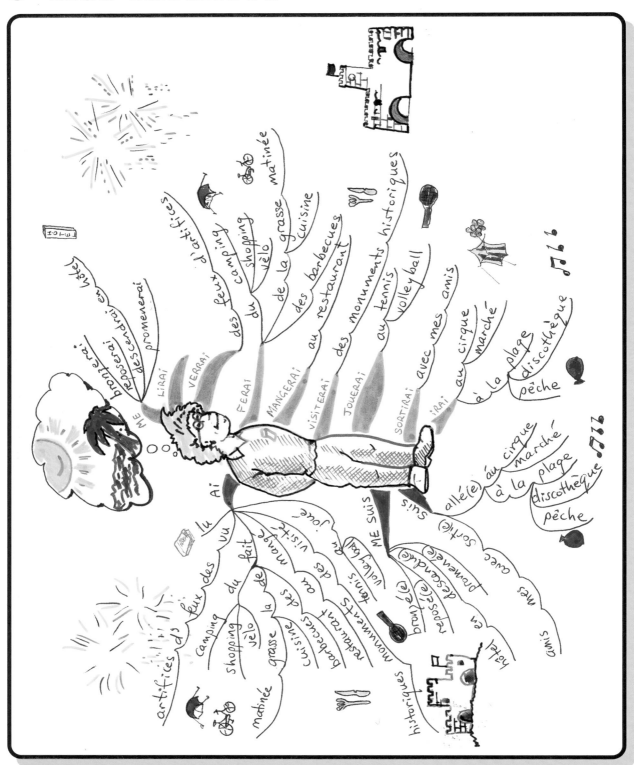

5 Mes vacances

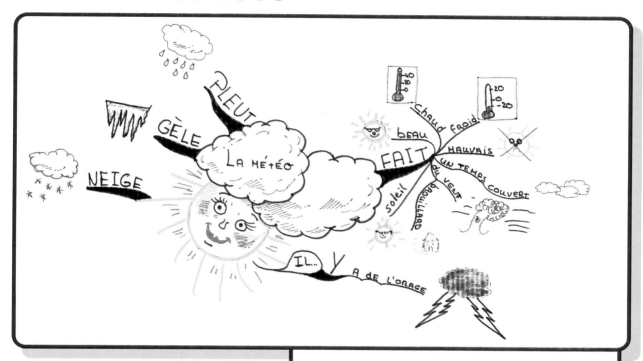

quel temps fait-il? = what's the weather like?

geler = to freeze
neiger = to snow
pleuvoir = to rain

le nuage = cloud
le temps = weather

la glace = ice
la météo = weather forecast

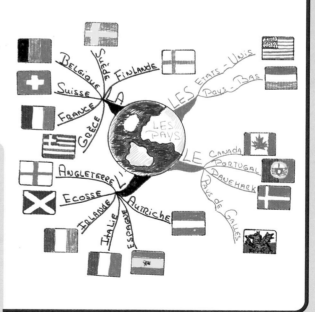

je suis allé(e) en France (en for feminine country)
je suis allé(e) au Portugal (au for masculine country)
je suis allé(e) aux Etats-Unis (aux for plural country)

6 En ville

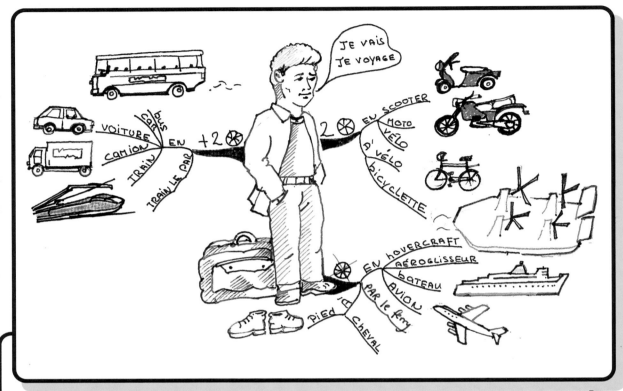

6 En ville

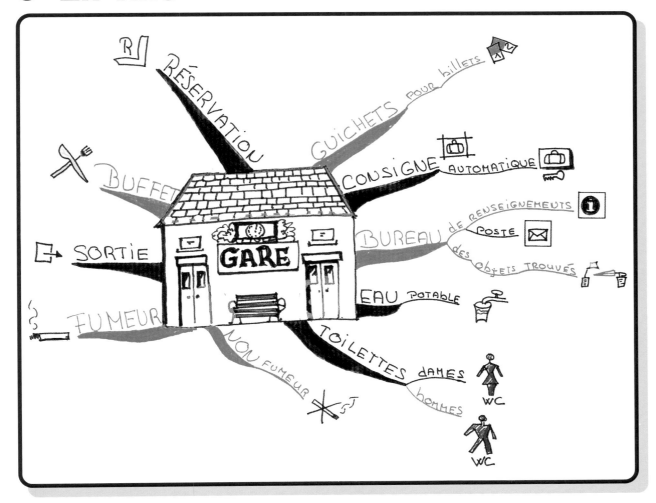

je prends	le bus
	le car
	le train
	le bateau
	le ferry
je prends	la voiture

tournez à droite = **turn right**
tournez à gauche = **turn left**
aller tout droit = **go straight ahead**
traversez ... = **cross ...**

je voudrais un aller simple à Paris en première classe
je voudrais un aller-retour à Paris en deuxième classe

N'OUBLIEZ PAS DE COMPOSTER VOTRE BILLET
 = **don't forget to stamp your ticket**
DEPARTS – GRANDES LIGNES
 = **main line / intercity departures**
DEPARTS BANLIEUES = **local departures**
c'est direct? = **is it direct?**
QUAIS = **platforms**
ACCES AUX QUAIS = **to the trains**
IL EST INTERDIT DE TRAVERSER LA VOIE
 = **it is forbidden to cross the track**
CORRESPONDANCES = **connections**
EN PROVENANCE DE ... = **trains coming from ...**
A DESTINATION DE ... = **trains going to ...**
INDICATEURS / HORAIRES = **timetables**

7 On fait des achats

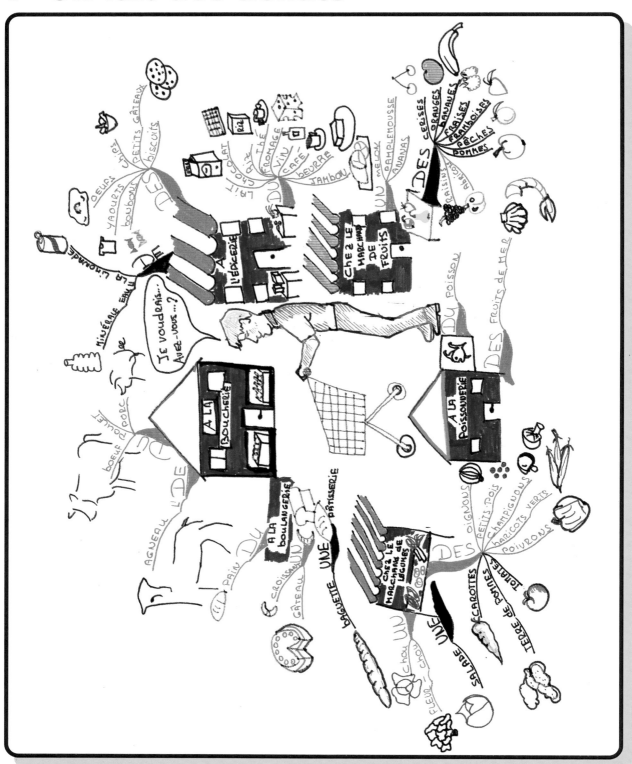

7 On fait des achats

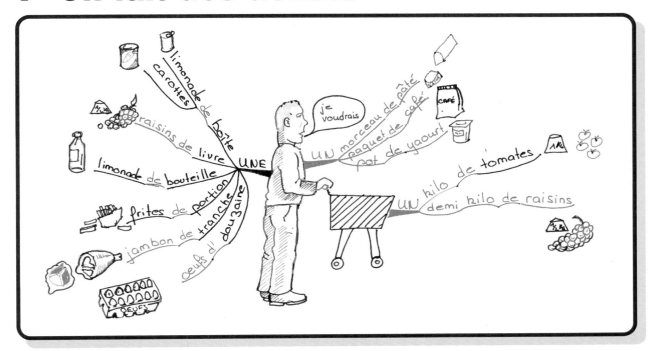

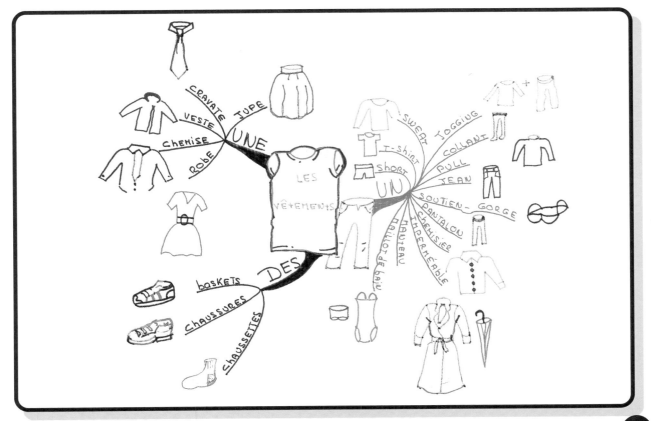

7 On fait des achats

8 Au café / Au restaurant

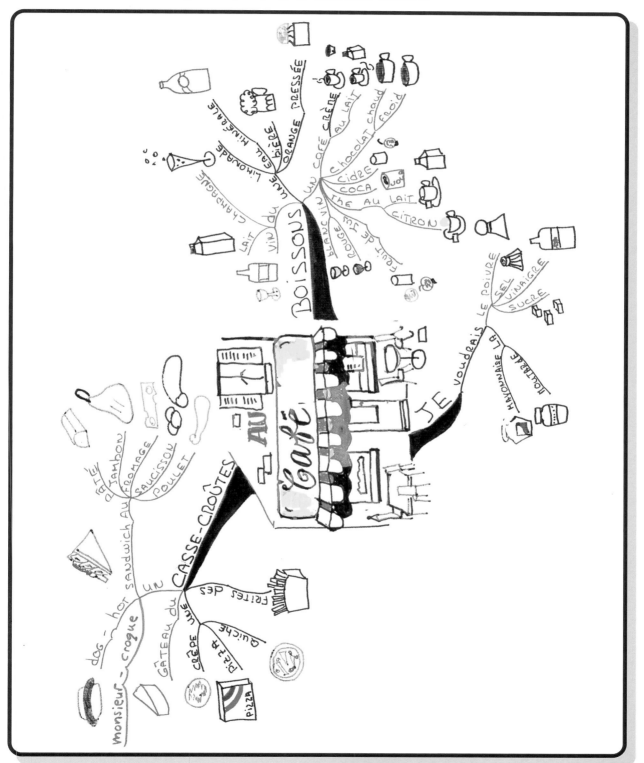

8 Au café / Au restaurant

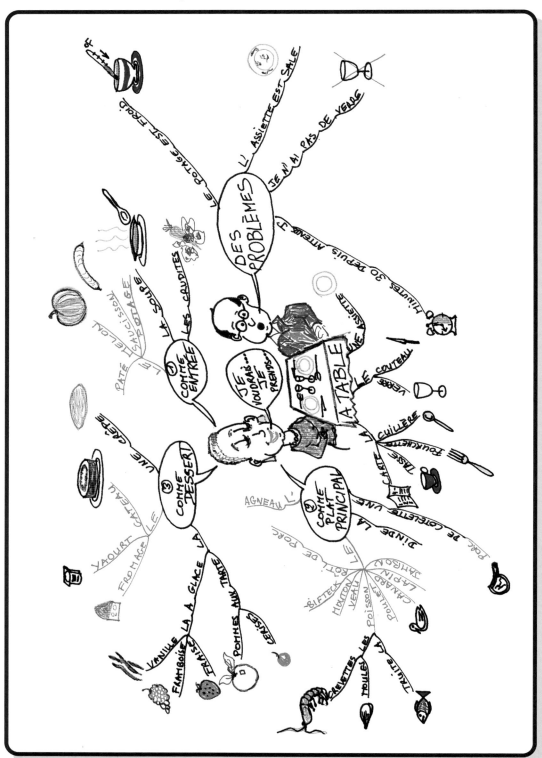

je service est compris? = is service included?
je voudrais commander = I'd like to order
je peux voir la carte s'il vous plaît? = can I see the menu please?

je voudrais = I would like
avez-vous ...? = have you got ...?
où sont les toilettes? = where are the toilets?
l'addition s'il vous plaît? = the bill please

9 Au collège

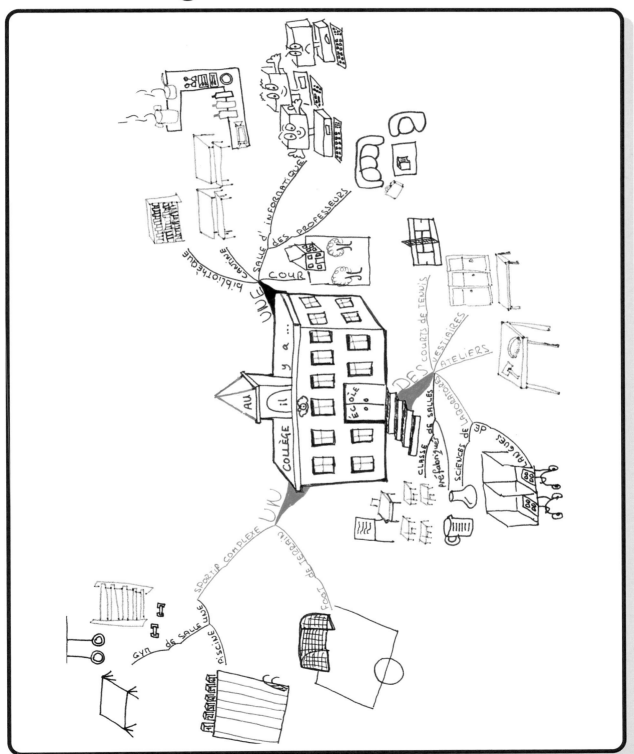

9 Au collège

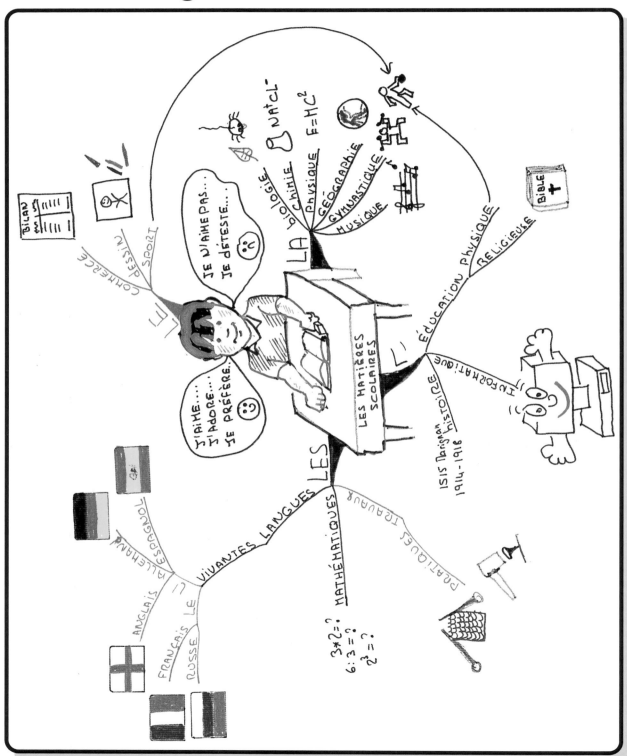

10 Au travail

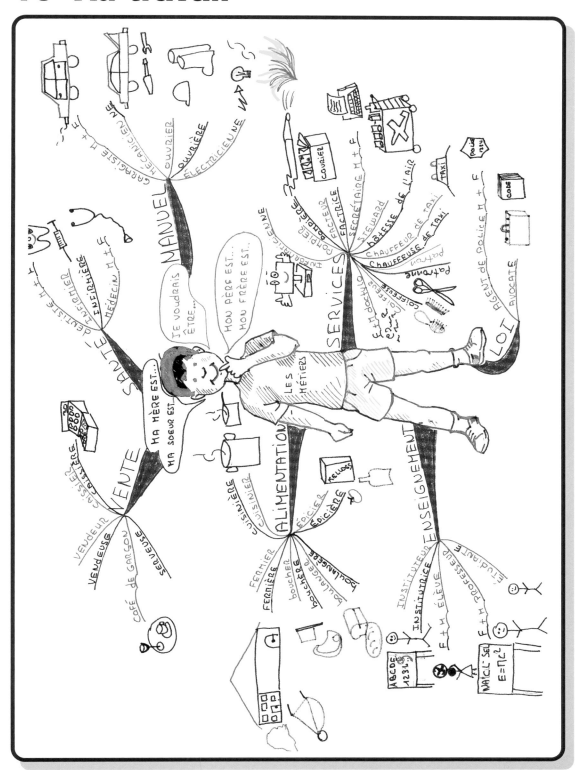

je suis au chomage = I'm unemployed
il / elle est = he / she is unemployed

The international world

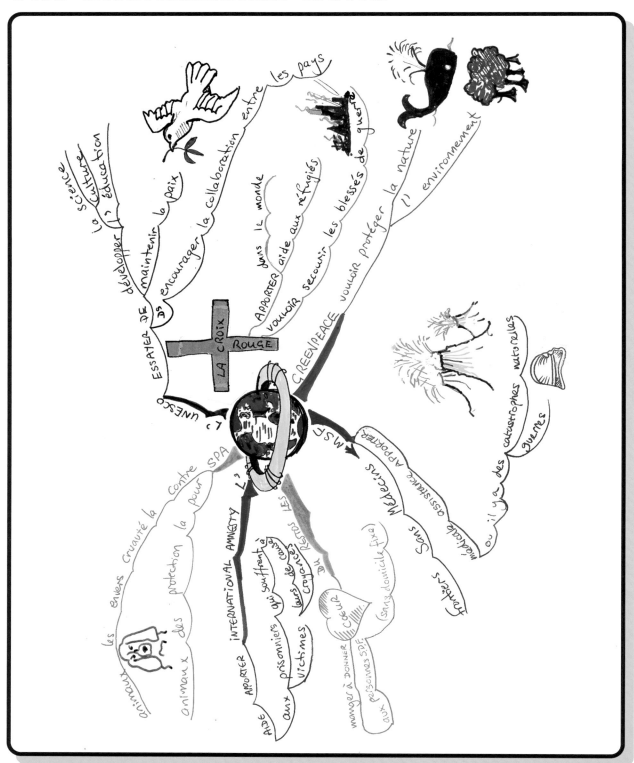

The international world

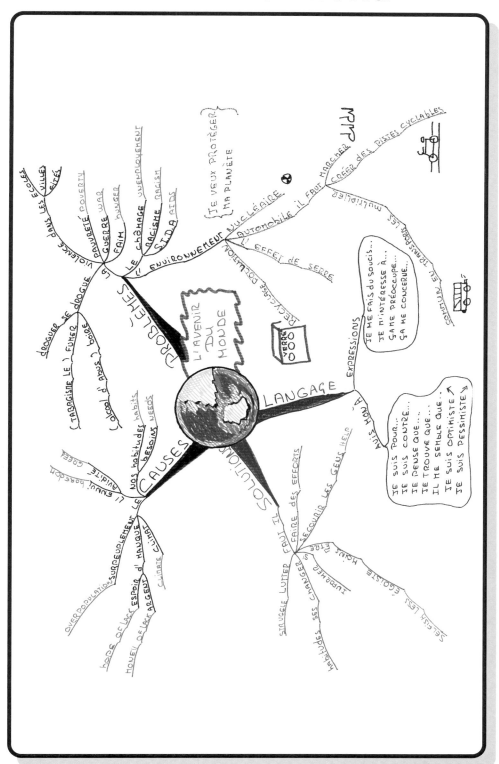

apporter l'aide = to bring help / assistance
secourir = to help
maintenir = to maintain
guérir = to cure
menacer = to threaten
soigner les malades = to care for the sick
tuer = to kill
éliminer = to eliminate
protéger = to protect

le tiers monde = third world
le pays = country
les pays en voie de développement =
developing countries
les droits = rights

la souffrance = suffering
la guerre = war

la religion
la paix = peace
la catastrophe
la victime
la faim = hunger
la pénurie (d'eau) = shortage (of water)
la cruauté = cruelty
les croyances = beliefs
les SDF (sans domicile fixe) = homeless

General

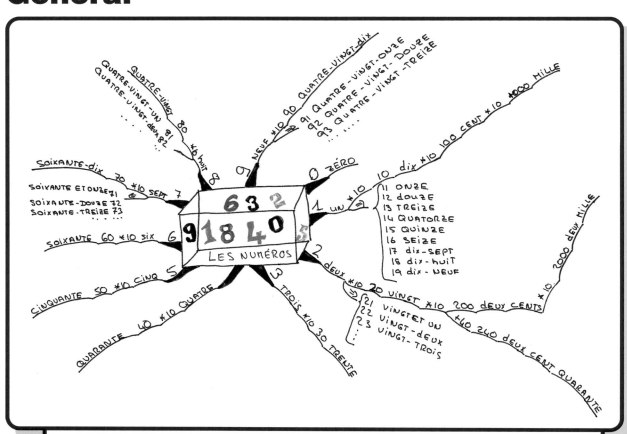

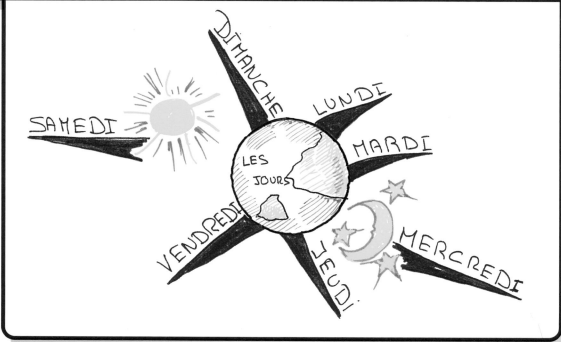

General

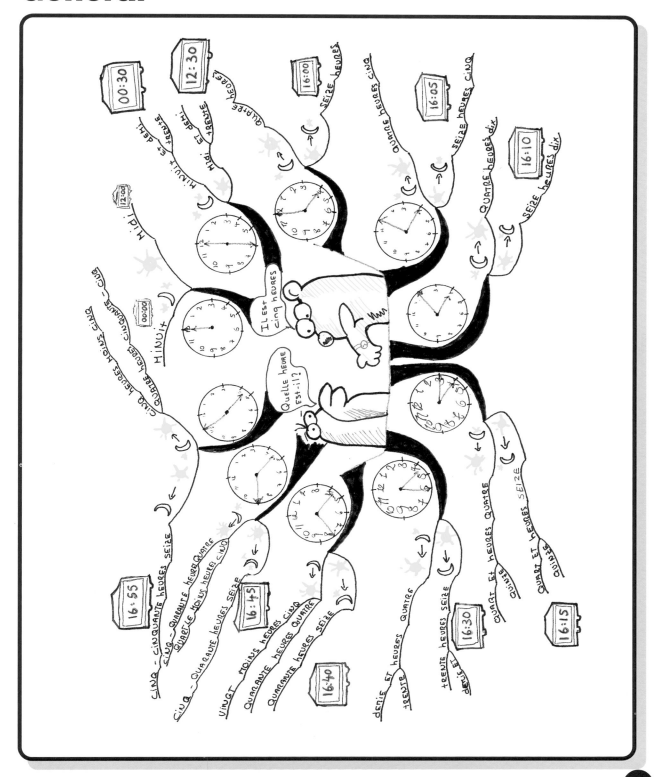

Grammar

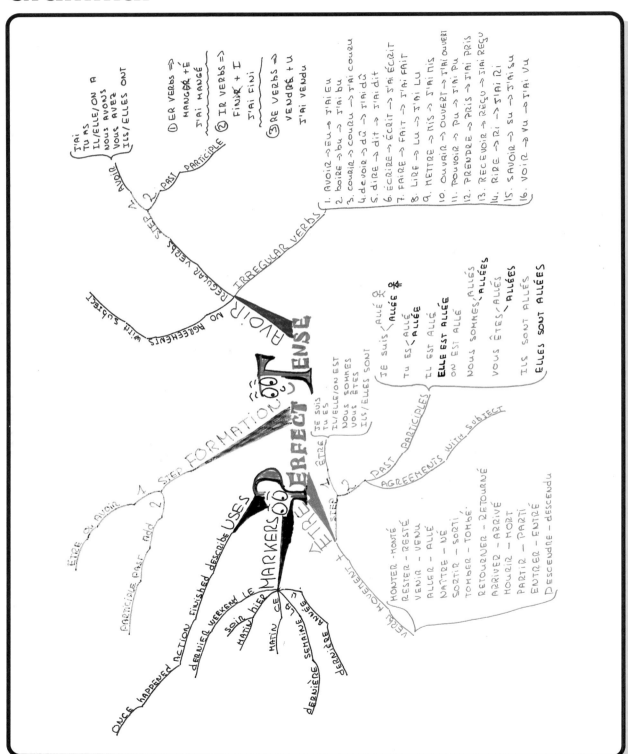

Grammar

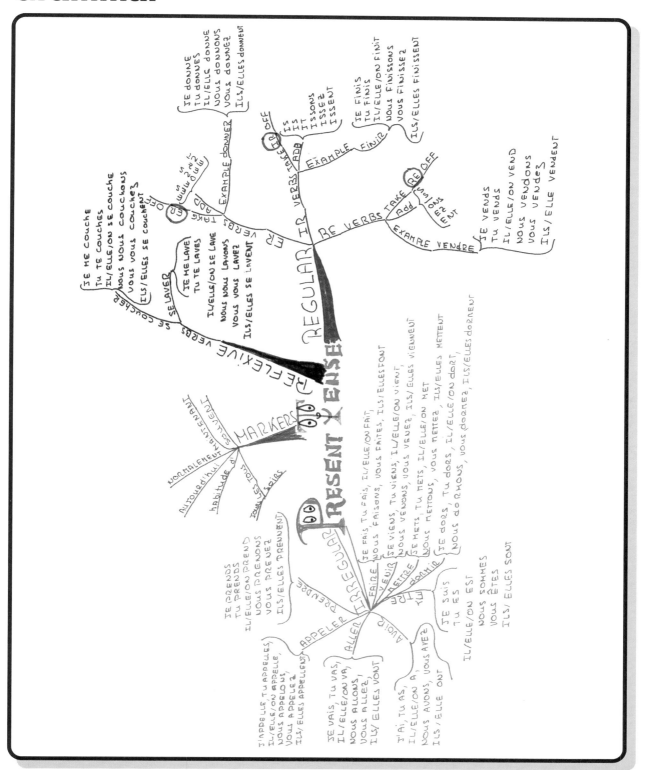

Grammar

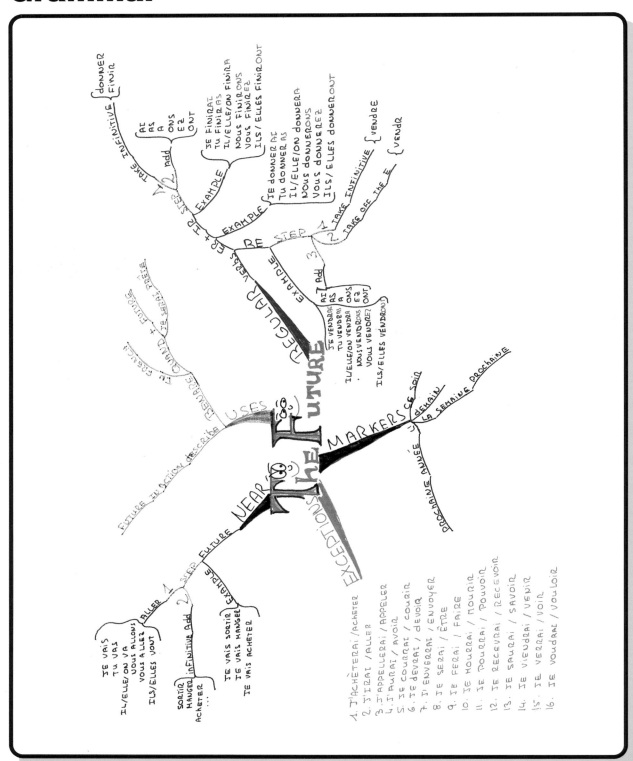

11 Mock exam paper

Before you start

The four exam papers covered here – there's one for each skill – each have three parts: if you are aiming for the Foundation tier, do the Foundation and Foundation / Higher parts, but if you are aiming for the Higher tier, do the Foundation / Higher and Higher parts.

But remember that in the exam you will get a booklet for the exam tier for which you have been entered: Foundation or Higher. So make sure you do all the activities in the examination booklet – don't miss anything out!

Make sure you know all the possible instructions listed on page 6.

The four skills

Listening

Ask your teacher to let you know whether the exam board with which you are entered allows you to use a dictionary – see page 8.

Your mock exam is on Side 2 of the cassette supplied with this study guide.

The pauses are timed so that you keep the cassette playing – don't stop it once you've started. You should also check with your teacher to see if the exam board with which you are entered uses timed pauses, or whether the teacher will stop the cassette for pauses.

On your cassette, the first part is the Foundation, then the Foundation / Higher and finally the Higher. So if you're doing the Higher tier, you'll have to fast forward to the start of the Foundation / Higher part.

Speaking

Give yourself 15 minutes to prepare your two role play activities using a dictionary. If you are entering a NEAB or MEG exam, prepare your Presentation. Record yourself if possible.

Reading

Use the dictionary that you will be using in your exam. Allow yourself approximately 50 minutes to complete the parts.

Writing

Only use the dictionary if you really need it. Check your work carefully. Allow yourself about an hour to complete the two parts.

Listening

Exercice 1 Au café

Choisissez la bonne image.
Ecrivez la lettre dans la case.

A   B C

D   E   F

G   H   I

J

Ecoutez l'exemple.

Exemple = [I]

1 = ☐

2 = ☐

3 = ☐ + ☐

4 = ☐ + ☐

[6]

125

Exercice 2 Les passe-temps

Ecoutez les préférences sportives de David, Mylène et André.

Cochez deux cases pour chaque personne.

Ecoutez l'exemple de David.

	🎾	⚽	🏊	🏃	⛵	🎣	🚴	⛷
David	✓							✓
Mylène								
André								

[4]

Exercise 3

You are going to Paris to stay with Anne, a French friend.

Answer each question by ticking one box only.

Example:

At the station
The train leaves from platform …?

A ☐

B ☐

C ☐

D ☑

1 At the station
How late is your train (in minutes)?

A ☐   B ☐   C ☐   D ☐

2 Meeting Anne
How does Anne suggest getting home?

A ☐   B ☐   C ☐   D ☐

3 At Anne's house
Anne asks if you would like to …?

A ☐   B ☐   C ☐   D ☐

4 At Anne's house
What does Anne suggest doing tonight?

A ☐    C ☐

B ☐    D ☐

[4]

Exercice 4

Vous allez entendre la météo pour la France deux fois.

Choisissez la bonne lettre pour chaque région.

A   B   C

D   E  F

G   H

Exemple: Normandie = __H__

1 Région Parisienne = ____

2 Massif Central = ____

3 Bretagne = ____

4 Alpes = ____

5 Languedoc = ____

6 Alsaçe = ____   [6]

Listening

Complete these exercises if you are doing the Foundation *or* the Higher tier.

Exercise 1

You are working in a hotel. A French person leaves a message on the answerphone to make a booking. Fill in the reservation details for your boss *in English*.

You will hear the message twice.

Name: Monsieur ....

Room details   double ☐   single ☐ (tick one)
                      shower ☐   bathroom ☐ (tick one)

Proposed dates of stay:

from .... to ....

Special requirements:

....

[4]

Exercice 2 Un échange scolaire

Vous allez entendre deux fois le programme d'activités d'un échange scolaire.

Complétez les notes en français.

Echange scolaire - programme d'activités	
lundi	*Plage* Départ à 9h 15 N'oubliez pas _____
mardi	*Réception officielle* Où? _____ Rendez-vous à _____ h _____
mercredi	*Journée en famille* Le soir, activité _____
jeudi	*Aqualand* Prix d'entrée _____ francs. Départ à 8h 30. Rendez-vous où? _____
vendredi	*Carcassonne – ville médiévale* Activités -i_____ -ii _____ N'oubliez pas _____
samedi	*Départ des Anglais* Rendez-vous à 15h 30. Où? _____

[10]

Exercice 3 Les vacances!

Vous allez entendre deux fois, deux jeunes, Marc et Nathalie.
Répondez aux questions en cochant la bonne case, A, B ou C.
D'abord, lisez les questions.

1 Nathalie est allée …

A ☐ en Espagne.

B ☐ à une station balnéaire.

C ☐ à la campagne.

2 Nathalie et Catrine ont séjourné …

A ☐ dans un camping.

B ☐ dans un petit appartement.

C ☐ dans une auberge de jeunesse.

3 Au début de leurs vacances, il a fait …

A ☐ beau.

B ☐ froid.

C ☐ un temps orageux.

4 Nathalie dit que l'année dernière, les prix des locations étaient …

A ☐ raisonnables.

B ☐ bon marché.

C ☐ chers.

5 Le matin, Nathalie et Catrine …

A ☐ restaient au lit.

B ☐ allaient à la plage.

C ☐ se promenaient en ville.

6 Selon Nathalie, quel était le seul inconvénient des vacances?

A ☐ Elles étaient loin de la mer.

B ☐ Les restaurants fermaient de bonne heure.

C ☐ Elles logeaient dans un quartier bruyant.

[6]

Listening

Complete these exercises only if you are doing the Higher tier.

Exercice 1 Le surf – la mode de la glisse

Vous allez entendre deux fois une interview avec Jérémy.
Il habite et surfe à la Martinique.
C'est vrai ou faux? Cochez la bonne case et corrigez les erreurs.

	Vrai	Faux
Exemple Jérémy surfe depuis l'âge de 3 ans.	☐	☑

Il surfe depuis l'âge de deux ans.

	Vrai	Faux
1 Son père s'appelle Morey.	☐	☐
2 Jérémy aime la sensation de vitesse dans ce sport.	☐	☐
3 Il s'entraîne tous les jours à la Martinique.	☐	☐
4 Il pratique aussi le surf des neiges depuis plusieurs années.	☐	☐
5 Le surf des neiges est plus difficile que le surf.	☐	☐
6 Il s'intéresse peu à la mode du surf.	☐	☐

[10]

Exercise 2

Here is Angélique talking about her search for work. You will hear her twice.

Answer the questions in English.

1 When Angélique was at school, where was she sent on work experience?

2 What did she like about her temporary job at the hospital?

3 How did she feel when she left?
  i   disappointed
  ii   _____

4 What does she say is the hardest thing about being out of work?

[4]

Exercice 3

Vous allez entendre, deux fois, trois jeunes, Cathy, Sylvain et Martine. Ils parlent de l'argent.

Encerclez la bonne réponse.

Regardez l'exemple.

Exemple:
Cathy reçoit (50 / 100 / 200) francs par semaine.

Cathy
1 Cathy trouve que 50 francs est (assez / peu raisonnable / trop).

2 A cause de l'argent, elle s'est disputée avec (son copain / son amie / ses parents).

Sylvain
3 Sylvain (ne reçoit jamais d'argent / reçoit de l'argent de temps en temps / reçoit de l'argent régulièrement).

4 Sylvain voudrait (chercher du travail / quitter le foyer / discuter avec ses parents).

Martine
5 Martine est plus (mûre / déprimée / fière) que Cathy et Sylvain.

Justifiez votre résponse.

_____

_____

[6]

Answers

Listening / Foundation

Exercise 1
1 = F; 2 = E; 3 = H + D (any order);
4 = B + A (any order) [6]

Exercise 2
Mylène tick: cycling and swimming
André tick: football and sailing [4]

Exercise 3
1 = C; 2 = B; 3 = A; 4 = C [4]

Exercise 4
1 = C; 2 = G; 3 = E; 4 = A; 5 = F; C = D [6]

Listening / Foundation + Higher

Exercise 1
1 = ROCHE
2 = double ✓ ; bathroom ✓
3 = 9th to 13th of July
4 = balcony + room on 1st floor [4]

Exercise 2
lundi = maillot
mardi = mairie + 18h 30
mercredi = disco (dancer)
jeudi = 115 francs; la poste (devant)
vendredi = visiter le château + faire du shopping;
pique-nique
samedi = aéroport [10] (1 mark for each item)

Exercise 3
1 = B; 2 = B; 3 = C; 4 = C; 5 = A;
6 = C [9]

Listening / Higher

Exercise 1
1 Faux : Sa planche s'appelait Morey.   1 + 1
2 Vrai   1
3 Faux : le mercredi et le week-end   1 + 1
4 Faux : depuis 1 an or il a fait du surf des neiges /   1 + 1
l'année dernière pour la première fois.
5 Faux : Le surf est plus difficile or Le surf   1 + 1
des neiges est moins difficile
6 Vrai [10]

129

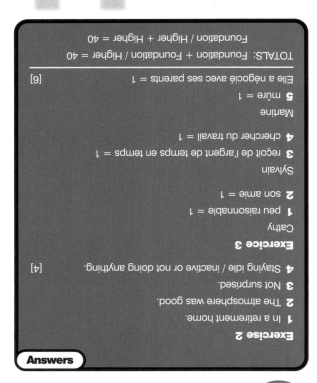

Answers

Exercice 2

1 In a retirement home.
2 The atmosphere was good.
3 Not surprised.
4 Staying idle / inactive or not doing anything. [4]

Exercice 3

Cathy
1 peu raisonnable = 1
2 son amie = 1
Sylvain
3 reçoit de l'argent de temps en temps = 1
4 chercher du travail = 1
Martine
5 mûre = 1
Elle a négocié avec ses parents = 1 [6]

TOTALS: Foundation + Foundation / Higher + Higher = 40
Foundation / Higher + Higher = 40

Speaking

Give yourself 15 minutes to prepare the two role play activities.

Candidate's role: You are in a French café, ordering a snack.
Your teacher will play the part of the waiter / waitress and will start the conversation.

	Teacher
1	Bonjour Monsieur/ Mademoiselle.

Dites ce que vous voulez.

2	Voilà et avec ça?

Posez la question.

Oui nous en avons au fromage, au jambon et au pâté.

3

Dites ce que vous voulez.

4

D'accord et comme boisson?

Dites ce que vous voulez.

5

Très bien.

Posez la question.

Oui, au fond du couloir.

Speaking

Candidate's role: You have lost a sports bag on a train and you go to the lost property office. Your teacher will play the part of the employee and will start the conversation.

	Teacher
	Bonjour je peux vous aider?
1 Saluez l'employé(e) et expliquez ce que vous avez perdu.	
	Pouvez-vous me décrire le sac?
2 Décrivez le sac (2 détails).	Où avez-vous perdu le sac?
3 Répondez à la question de l'employé(e).	A quelle heure?
4 Dites quand vous avez perdu le sac.	D'accord. Et qu'est-ce qu'il y avait dans le sac?
5 Décrivez ce qu'il y avait dans le sac (2 détails).	Bon, je vais voir si on l'a trouvé.

Speaking

H

EITHER (ULEAC type)

You see this advertisement for a job on a children's summer camp and ring up to give details about yourself. You have some experience of this kind of work.

> **COLONIE DE VACANCES**
> **ETE 98**
> **RECHERCHE**
> **MONITEURS/MONITRICES**
>
> **BON NIVEAU EN ANGLAIS**
> **ET FRANCAIS**

Teacher's questions

1 Pouvez-vous me donner vos détails personnels. Nom? Age? Nationalité?

2 Parlez-vous des langues étrangères? - couramment?

3 Quelle expérience avez-vous de ce travail? Où? Quand?

4 Quand pouvez-vous travailler?

OR (MEG type)

The notes and pictures below give an outline of the preparations for your birthday party last year.

Tell the examiner what happened. You need not mention every detail but you must cover the whole day's events.

Qu'est-ce que vous avez fait?

Où êtes-vous allé(e)?

Comment? Avec qui? Pourquoi?

Rentrer à la maison. Qu'est-ce que vous avez fait?

Vos parents? Qu'est-ce qu'ils ont fait?

A quelle heure?

Qui est arrivé chez vous?

Qu'avez-vous fait?

Vos parents Etaient-ils contents?

Et vous? Qu'est-ce que vous avez fait?

Se coucher à quelle heure?

Reading

Exercice 1   On fait du shopping!

Choisissez le bon magasin (A – H).
Ecrivez la bonne lettre.

Exemple:

   = C

1    = _____

2    = _____

3    = _____

4    = _____

5    = _____

6    = _____

Magasins

A BOULANGERIE	F CHARCUTERIE
B PATISSERIE	G PHARMACIE
C POISSONNERIE	H LIBRAIRIE
D TABAC	I BIJOUTERIE
E EPICERIE	J BOUCHERIE [6]

Answers

Speaking / Foundation

1 Je voudrais / une portion de / des frites.
2 Avez-vous des sandwichs?
3 Je voudrais un sandwich au jambon.
4 Je voudrais une limonade et un café.
5 Est-ce qu'il y a des toilettes? / Où sont les toilettes?

Speaking / Foundation + Higher

1 J'ai perdu un sac de sports.
2 Il est / (+ colour such as noir / marron / bleu) (+ size such as grand / petit – other details acceptable).
3 J'ai perdu le sac dans un train.
4 J'ai perdu le sac à (+ time).
5 Il y avait (+ two details such as mon appareil / des vêtements / un porte-feuille).

Speaking / Higher

1 Je m'appelle _____. J'ai _____ ans. Je suis anglais(e).
2 Je parle anglais et français (allemand / espagnol) couramment / depuis cinq ans.
3 J'ai travaillé dans une colonie en Angleterre l'année dernière (other places / dates acceptable). Be prepared to give extra appropriate details!
4 Je peux / pourrai travailler du (+ date) au (+ date).

OR

L'année dernière, j'ai fêté mon anniversaire. J'ai décidé de faire une boum, alors j'ai téléphoné à mes amis pour les inviter. Après avoir téléphoné à mes amis, je suis allé(e) au supermarché faire des courses avec ma famille. J'ai acheté des boissons et de la nourriture. J'y suis allé(e) en voiture. Puis, on est rentré à la maison avec les provisions. Ensuite, j'ai nettoyé la maison et j'ai fait des préparatifs pour la boum – j'ai fait la cuisine, j'ai préparé des pizzas. A huit heures, mes parents sont sortis au restaurant et je me suis préparé(e). A neuf heures, mes amis sont arrivés chez moi et on a commencé à faire la fête! On a mis des CD. J'ai dansé, j'ai bavardé avec mes copains et j'ai mangé. C'était chouette, il y avait une bonne ambiance. Plus tard, mes parents sont rentrés. Ils n'étaient pas très contents parce que la maison était en désordre et il y avait beaucoup de bruit! Alors j'ai dû nettoyer la maison et tout remettre en ordre. Deux heures plus tard, j'étais crevé(e) / fatigué(e) et je me suis couché(e). C'était quand même une très bonne soirée et une boum réussie!

Exercice 2 On fait du sport!

Cochez la bonne case.

Exemple:

dimanche =  A ☑ B ☐ C ☐

Centre Aéré de Brignais

Programme:		
	dimanche	tournoi de tennis
	lundi	planche à voile
	mardi	stage de vélo
	mercredi	tournoi de pêche
	jeudi	promenade à cheval
	vendredi	stage de voile
	samedi	natation

1 lundi =  A ☐ B ☐ C ☐

2 mardi =  A ☐ B ☐ C ☐

3 mercredi =  A ☐ B ☐ C ☐

4 jeudi =  A ☐ B ☐ C ☐

5 vendredi =  A ☐ B ☐ C ☐

6 samedi =  A ☐ B ☐ C ☐

[6]

Exercise 3

CIRQUE PINDER

du 2 août – 16 août

◆ Achetez deux places et la troisième place est **gratuite**!

◆ Présentez-vous aux caisses du cirque avec ce papier avant 17 heures.

Horaires des séances d'été.
Matinée 18h (après la plage).
Soirée 21h 15.
Prix des places à partir de 65F.

Answer the questions in English.

1 What do you get if you buy two circus tickets?

2 What should you take with you to get the special offer?

3 By what time do you have to arrive at the ticket office?

4 What does the leaflet suggest that you might do **before** you go to a matinée performance?

[4]

Exercice 4

Vendredi à l'école.

C'est vrai ou c'est faux? Cochez la bonne case.

			Vrai	Faux
8.30 ⇓ 9.30		Exemple: Le premier cours commence à 8h 30.	☐	☑
⇓ récréation ⇓		**1** A 9h 30, c'est la géographie.	☐	☐
10.30 ⇓		**2** Après la récréation, c'est le dessin.	☐	☐
11.30 ⇓		**3** Avant le déjeuner, c'est le français.	☐	☐
PAUSE DEJEUNER ⇓ 14.00 ⇓ 15.00 ⇓ 16.00 ⇓ 17.00		**4** L'éducation physique finit à 16 heures.	☐	☐

[4]

133

Reading

Exercice 1

Lisez ces renseignements touristiques.

A

Les P'tits Mousses – Jeux
Club de Plage (2 – 10 ans)
Ouvert le 1er juillet
au 21 août

B

Cave Jean-Guy et
Bruno Arrivé
Pineau des Charentes
– Vins Fins

C

AVIS IMMOBILIER
2 rue Gaulté – St Gilles
Transactions immobilières –
locations

D

L'ami du Pêcheur
Promenade en mer
mardi et jeudi –
Port de Croix-de-Vie

E

MARCHÉ ARTISANAL
NOCTURNE
Place du Vieux Port
Pensez à vos cadeaux!

F

Promenade Pédestre
Visite guidée des ports de
pêche et de plaisance –
Inscription à l'Office de
Tourisme

G

Fête du 14 juillet
St Gilles Croix-de-Vie – défilé,
bal populaire feux d'artifice
à 22 h

H

Vivre le Moyen Age – 8 juillet
– 25 août
Au Château de Talmont
monument historique

Ecrivez la bonne lettre.

Exemple: Mon père veut déguster le vin.   B

1 Je voudrais me promener et visiter les quais.   _____

2 Mon ami veut louer un appartement.   _____

3 Mon petit frère veut jouer et s'amuser.   _____

4 Je voudrais danser et voir un spectacle.   _____

5 Je voudrais me promener en bateau.   _____

6 Ma mère veut acheter des souvenirs ce soir.   _____

[6]

Exercice 2

Lisez cette lettre.

> Toulon
> le 6 septembre
>
> Chère Axelle,
>
> J'espère que tu as passé de bonnes vacances à
> Biarritz; j'ai reçu ta carte - merci! Moi, j'ai passé
> le mois de juillet à travailler comme serveuse
> dans un café. C'était amusant, mais fatigant.
> Quand je ne travaillais pas je sortais avec mes
> copains. Le soir on allait en boîte et on se
> promenait dans le port - c'était chouette.
>
> En août je suis allée chez ma correspondante
> espagnole. On s'entendait assez bien, elle est
> sympa, mais j'ai eu du mal à comprendre la
> famille, surtout le frère qui parlait vite. En plus j'ai
> trouvé qu'on mange très tard, le soir, en Espagne
> - j'avais toujours faim. On a visité Barcelone et j'ai
> adoré la ville mais le voyage pour y aller était long!
>
> Demain, c'est la rentrée - je passe en première,
> j'aurai du travail à faire cette année!
>
> Ecris-moi vite.
>
> Sandrine

Cochez la case Vrai si l'affirmation est vraie.
Cochez la case Faux si l'affirmation est fausse et
corrigez l'affirmation en français.

Vrai Faux

Exemple:

Axelle a passé ses vacances à Paris.   ☐ ☑

Axelle a passé ses vacances à Biarritz.

1 Sandrine est partie en vacances en juillet.   ☐ ☐

_____

2 Elle a travaillé à la caisse d'un café.   ☐ ☐

_____

3 En juillet, Sandrine est allée danser.   ☐ ☐

_____

4 Elle ne comprenait pas le frère de sa correspondante. ☐ ☐

_____

5 Elle avait faim en Espagne parce qu'elle n'aimait pas la nourriture. ☐ ☐

_____

6 Sandrine est rentrée en France pour travailler. ☐ ☐

[10]

_____

Exercise 3

Read this article and answer the questions in English.

Plus d'école l'après-midi

Matières scolaires le matin, sport et activités culturelles l'après-midi ....; à la prochaine rentrée scolaire, plus de 200 villes testeront ces nouveaux rythmes scolaires. L'objectif est de permettre aux enfants de s'épanouir davantage mais aussi d'aménager des journées moins fatigantes. Les établissements scolaires concernés sont surtout des écoles primaires. Mais des collèges participeront aussi à l'expérience. Si ça marche, peut-être qu'un jour toutes les écoles adopteront ces nouvelles journées.

1 From next September, what will some pupils be doing in the afternoons?

i .... ii ....

2 How many towns will take part in the experiment?

....

3 One of the aims of this experiment is (choose one):

A ☐ to make the school day less tiring.

B ☐ to close the schools at lunchtime.

C ☐ to employ fewer teaching staff.

4 Most of the schools in this experiment are

....

[4]

Reading

Exercise 1

Read this letter to a magazine.
Answer the questions in English.

Mes parents

Je trouve mes parents assez cools. Seulement, j'ai toujours peur de les décevoir alors je dois parfois mentir. Je sais qu'ils s'inquiètent beaucoup pour moi car je suis restée longtemps sans copines. Depuis que je suis au collège ça va mieux mais j'ai souvent le blues. Ma mère est accro aux notes du collège et mon père veut que je réussisse dans la musique. Ils se disputent souvent, disant que soit la musique soit l'école est le plus important. Moi, je suis coincée car il faudrait que je réussisse partout sinon l'un des deux est sur mon dos jusqu'aux prochaines vacances. (Clotilde – 15 ans)

1 Why does Clotilde feel that she sometimes has to lie to her parents?

2 What made her parents worry about her when she was at junior school?

3 Why do Clotilde's parents argue?

4 How does Clotilde feel about the present situation?

[4]

Exercice 2

Lisez cet article.

La natation synchronisée

Marianne Aeschbacher est une des championnes françaises les plus titrées .... Aujourd'hui, elle prépare les Jeux Olympiques ....

Okapi: A quel âge avez-vous commencé à pratiquer la natation synchronisée?

Marianne: A 9 ans. Je faisais de la danse classique et de la natation sportive. Comme je ne pouvais plus faire les deux, j'ai choisi un sport qui alliait les deux disciplines. En natation synchronisée, il vaut mieux commencer tôt et il faut être patient, car ce sport demande beaucoup d'efforts.

Okapi: Tout en menant votre carrière sportive vous n'avez jamais délaissé les études ....

Marianne: Il faut préparer sa sortie du sport. C'est une question d'équilibre aussi. Quand ça ne marche pas sur le plan sportif, ça permet de prendre du recul.

Okapi: Vous arrêtez votre carrière après les Jeux Olympiques. N'est-ce pas trop dur d'admettre qu'à 25 ans, pour ce sport, on est déjà vieille.

Marianne: Si, bien sûr. Mais, j'ai des souvenirs formidables, j'ai fait de superbes voyages. Mais l'essentiel c'est de ne jamais oublier que ce qui compte avant tout, c'est de se faire plaisir bien plus que les résultats.

Cochez la bonne case.

1 Pourquoi Marianne a-t-elle choisi de faire de la natation synchronisée?

Elle n'arrivait pas à nager très rapidement.	A ☐
Elle voulait combiner ses deux sports préférés.	B ☐
Elle ne voulait plus faire de danse classique.	C ☐

2 Il vaut mieux commencer ce sport tôt car . . .

il faut du temps pour réussir.	A ☐
il faut être petite de taille.	B ☐
il faut être souple.	C ☐

3 Que dit-elle à propos de son mode de vie?

Elle a laissé tomber ses études.	A ☐
Le sport est la chose la plus importante dans sa vie.	B ☐
Il faut qu'elle pense à son avenir.	C ☐

4 Comment Marianne a-t-elle profité de ses expériences?

Elle a rencontré beaucoup de jeunes.	A ☐
Elle a eu de bons résultats.	B ☐
Elle s'est bien amusée.	C ☐

[4]

Exercice 3

Lisez cet article au sujet du papier recyclé. Pour chaque blanc, indiquez le mot qui manque. Attention il y a des mots supplémentaires!

Exemple: 1 = quantité.

Papier recyclé

Vieux papiers deviendront neufs.

8 millions de tonnes. C'est la (1) _____ de papier utilisée chaque année en France. Seulement, 36% des journaux, des livres, des emballages, des cahiers sont (2) _____ . C'est dommage, car le recyclage a beaucoup d'avantages.

Pour fabriquer la pâte à papier il (3) _____ des fibres en bois. En France on (4) _____ les déchets des scieries et tout ce qui (5) _____ de l'entretien des bois. Mais on utilise aussi beaucoup d'arbres. Pour fabriquer tout le papier dont nous avons (6) _____ la France fait venir de la pâte canadienne et (7) _____ . Le bois utilisé par ces pays est d'une grande valeur (8) _____ . Si on utilisait (9) _____ de papier recyclé ces milieux naturels seraient préservés. Récupérer tous les vieux papiers est le seul problème. Le papier représente 30% de nos déchets (10) _____ et seuls 3% finissent dans le recyclage. Il faut (11) _____ un peu plus d'efforts. Alors, à vos poubelles!

Voici les mots qui manquent:

faut	davantage	utilise
suédoise	besoin	quantité
faire	recyclés	écologique
ménagers	vient	Canada
nucléaires	minérale	moins

[5]

Exercice 4

Lisez cet article.

Qu'avez-vous fait de vos 15 ans?

Françoise Giroud, Ancien ministre, journaliste

A 15 ans, je travaillais déjà depuis un an. J'étais sténo-dactylo et vendeuse dans une librairie. Je n'avais pas le choix. Ma mère avait été ruinée par la mort de mon père, j'ai donc dû quitter l'école. C'était très difficile, mais à 15 ans, on a du ressort.

J'avais passé trois mois dans une école pour apprendre la dactylo, je ne voulais pas rester vendeuse toute ma vie..... Je ne rêvais d'aucun métier précis, j'avais depuis longtemps renoncé à mon désir d'être médecin, les études coûtant bien trop chères. Il y avait tout de même un avantage à travailler dans une librairie: J'ai lu tout le magasin, de Balzac à Tolstoï, par ordre alphabétique!

Mes distractions étaient réduites au minimum. J'étais très solitaire. Ma soeur aînée me tenait lieu d'amie. Quant aux garçons, je ne m'y intéressais pas, à une exception près: j'étais amoureuse depuis l'âge de 10 ans du réalisateur Marc Allégret, qui était un ami de ma famille. C'est aussi grâce à lui que l'année suivante, j'ai quitté la librairie, en devenant scripte pour un de ses films.

Répondez aux questions **en français**.

1 A quel âge Françoise a-t-elle commencé à travailler?

2 Pourquoi a-t-elle dû quitter l'école?

3 Pourquoi a-t-elle appris la dactylo?

4 Pourquoi n'est-elle pas devenue médecin?

5 Quel était son passe-temps préféré?

6 En parlant de ses distractions elle dit qu'elle (cochez une case).
A ☐ avait peu d'amies.
B ☐ sortait souvent avec des garçons.
C ☐ ne s'entendait pas avec les garçons.
D ☐ ne s'entendait pas avec sa soeur.

7 Après avoir travaillé à la librairie, qu'est-ce qu'elle a fait?

[7]

Answers

Reading / Foundation

Exercice 1
1 = A; 2 = I; 3 = E; 4 = F; 5 = B; 6 = G [6]

Exercice 2
1 = B; 2 = A; 3 = A; 4 = C; 5 = B; 6 = B [6]

Exercice 3
1 3rd ticket free
2 This piece of paper / leaflet
3 Before 17h (5 pm)
4 Go to the beach [4]

Exercice 4
1 Vrai; 2 Vrai; 3 Faux; 4 Faux [4]

TOTAL = [20]

Reading / Foundation + Higher

Exercice 1
1 = F; 2 = C; 3 = A; 4 = G; 5 = D; 6 = E [6]

Exercice 2
1 Faux. Elle a travaillé en juillet or Elle est partie en août.
2 Faux. Elle a travaillé comme serveuse.
3 Vrai. 4 Vrai.
5 Faux. On mange très tard en Espagne.
6 Faux. Elle est rentrée/pour aller à l'école/or c'est la rentrée scolaire. [10]

Exercice 3
1 sports / ii cultural activities
2 More than 200
3 A
4 Primary / Junior schools [4]

TOTAL = [20]

Reading / Higher

Exercice 1
1 So that she won't disappoint them/let them down.
2 She had no friends.
3 One says (father) that music is more important, the other that her school work is more important.
4 She feels trapped/caught between the two of them, has to do well in everything. [4]

Exercice 2
1 = B; 2 = A; 3 = C; 4 = C [4]

137

Answers

Exercice 3

(2) recyclés **(3)** faut **(4)** utilise **(5)** vient
(6) besoin **(7)** suédoise **(8)** écologique
(9) davantage **(10)** ménagers **(11)** faire

$10 \div 2 = [5]$

Exercice 4

1 14 ans
2 Son père est mort/Pour gagner de l'argent.
3 Elle ne voulait pas rester vendeuse toute sa vie.
4 Les études étaient/coûtaient trop chères.
5 la lecture/lire   **6** a
7 Elle a travaillé comme scripte pour Marc Allégret *not* elle a tourné un film.   [7]

TOTAL = [20]

Writing

Exercice 1

Vous cherchez un correspondant.
Remplissez ce formulaire en français.

Nom:	1
Nationalité:	1
Date de naissance: le .... mois 19	1
Sport préféré:	1
Autres passe-temps. i	1
ii	1
Plat préféré:	1
Boisson préférée	1
Couleur des cheveux:	1
Matières d'école préférées: i............................	1
ii	1

[10]

Exercice 2

Vous êtes en vacances.

Ecrivez une carte postale (40 mots) à votre ami(e).

Dites

- où vous êtes

- avec qui vous êtes

- où vous logez

- ce que vous faites (deux activités)

[10]

Writing

Exercice 1

Vous avez reçu une lettre d'une amie française – Axelle.
Ecrivez une réponse à Axelle.
Répondez à toutes ses questions (100 mots).

> Torreilles
>
> le 9 septembre
>
> Salut!
>
> Ça va? J'espère que tu as passé de bonnes vacances. Qu'est-ce que tu as fait, et avec qui? Est-ce que tu as travaillé pendant les vacances – moi, j'ai eu de la chance et j'ai trouvé du travail dans un café. Quels sont tes projets pour Noël? Ma mère voudrait t'inviter à passer 15 jours ici chez nous. Qu'en penses-tu?
>
> Réponds-moi vite!
>
> Ton amie,
>
> Axelle

[20]

Writing

Exercice 1

Vous voyez un débat dans un magazine.

Débat

Que pensez-vous de votre ville / village?
Participez à notre débat.
Ecrivez vos réponses à nos questions.

- Où habitez-vous?
- Décrivez les avantages d'habiter votre ville/village.
- Décrivez les inconvénients de votre ville/village.
- Aimez-vous habiter votre ville/village? Pourquoi/pas?

Ecrivez une réponse au magazine (150 mots maximum). [20]

Answers

Writing / Foundation

Exercice 1

anglais / anglaise / le + date (figures acceptable) janvier, etc. (see page 124 to revise months) :
le tennis / foot / badminton / rugby, etc. – accept any sport / accept the name of any other pastimes such as (la) danse / danser, vélo / 'faire du vélo, lecture / lire, etc:
plat préféré – accept any main course such as la viande, le poisson, le poulet / boisson préférée – accept any drink, le café / le thé / le coca, etc:
couleur des cheveux – any sensible colour acceptable:
any two school subjects acceptable.
Each item = 1 if the message is put across – the spelling does not have to be perfect but recognisable!

10 × 1 = [10]

Exercice 2

- Je suis à + name / en France / au bord de la mer.
- avec ma famille / mes amis.
- Je reste / séjourne à l'hôtel / dans un camping, etc.
- Je nage et je joue au volley.

Amitiés ....

Each task successfully completed (message understood fully) = 2

5 × 2 = [10]

Answers

Writing / Foundation + Higher

Different exam boards have different ways of marking at this level. Basically between one-third and one half of the marks are available for Communication (i.e. answering the set tasks / questions in the letter) and the remaining marks are rewarded for the accuracy of the language you use and the way you use it.

Here is a model answer.

Chère Axelle,
Merci bien de ta lettre. Moi, aussi, j'ai passé de bonnes vacances. Je suis allée dans la région des lacs avec mes amis. On est resté dans des auberges de jeunesse. Je me suis promenée à la montagne et j'ai nagé dans les lacs. C'était chouette. Après mon séjour à Windermere j'ai travaillé dans un magasin près de chez moi.
J'aimerais beaucoup passer les vacances de Noël chez toi et je te remercie de l'invitation. Je pourrai venir du 20 décembre au 4 janvier. Ça va? Moi, j'attends les vacances avec impatience!
Ecris-moi vite
Caroline

Writing / Higher

Again, different exam boards mark the final question on the Higher Writing Paper in slightly different ways. Some marks are available for Communication but more marks are rewarded for the accuracy of the language you use and the way you use it. Try to be as accurate as possible if you want to gain high marks.

Here is a model answer.

Mon village
J'habite à la campagne dans un petit village pittoresque dans le sud-ouest de l'Angleterre à 20 km de la ville de Bath. Il y a deux mille habitants dans le village. Je trouve le paysage autour du village agréable. C'est une région rurale et agricole et j'aime habiter ici parce que c'est tranquille et il n'y a pas beaucoup de pollution. J'ai beaucoup d'amis dans le village. On fait du vélo et on va souvent faire du shopping à Bath. Il y a beaucoup de touristes à Bath car c'est une ville très historique avec beaucoup de monuments à visiter. On peut aussi aller au cinéma et au théâtre à Bath.
Il y a quand même des inconvénients pour les jeunes. Le soir, il n'y a rien à faire (il faut un club des jeunes) et la boîte la plus près est à dix kilomètres. Alors il est difficile de rentrer si on sort en boîte ou à Bath parce que les bus s'arrêtent à 8h du soir! J'aime habiter ici mais il n'y a pas assez de distractions pour les jeunes.

Grammar

12

Whether you are going to sit Foundation or Higher papers (or a mix of both), you will not only need to learn the vocabulary in the earlier chapters but also the grammatical rules which make French work. Some of the sections are marked **Active** which means you should be able to produce the structures (e.g. in Speaking and Writing). Other sections are marked **Receptive** which means you only need to recognise and understand them (e.g. in Reading and Listening). Sections are also marked F (Foundation) or H (Higher). If you are entered for the Foundation Tier, miss out the sections marked H Receptive and H Active.

Verbs

1 Present tense	**F + H** Active
2 Perfect tense	**F + H** Active
3 Imperfect tense	**F** Receptive / **H** Active
4 Future tense (and near Future)	**F + H** Active
5 Pluperfect tense	**H** Active
6 Past historic tense	**H** Receptive
7 Conditional tense	**F** Receptive / **H** Active
8 Conditional perfect tense	**H** Receptive
9 Venir de + infinitive	**F + H** Active
10 Present subjunctive	**H** Receptive
11 Present participle	**F** Receptive / **H** Active
12 Infinitives (using two verbs together)	**F** Receptive / **H** Active
13 Perfect infinitive	**F** Receptive / **H** Active
14 Negatives	**F + H** Active
15 Imperatives (giving orders)	**F** Receptive / **H** Active
16 Interrogatives (how to ask questions)	**F + H** Active
17 Passive voice	**H** Receptive

Nouns

1 Gender	**F + H** Active
2 Definite article	**F + H** Active
3 Indefinite article	**F + H** Active
4 Partitive article	**F + H** Active
5 Plurals	**F + H** Active
6 Possession	**F + H** Active

Adjectives

1 Formation and position	**F + H** Active
2 Possessive adjectives	**F + H** Active
3 Demonstrative adjectives	**F** Receptive / **H** Active
4 Comparative and superlative adjectives	**F + H** Active
5 Indefinite adjectives	**F + H** Active

Adverbs

1 Formation	**F + H** Active
2 Comparatives and superlatives	**F + H** Active

Pronouns

1 Subject pronouns	**F + H** Active
2 Direct object pronouns	**F + H** Active
3 Indirect object pronouns	**F + H** Active
4 En	**F + H** Active
5 Y	**F + H** Active
6 Position of pronouns	**F** Receptive / **H** Active
7 Emphatic pronouns	**F + H** Active
8 Relative pronouns	**F + H** Active
9 Interrogative pronouns	**F + H** Active
10 Demonstrative pronouns	**F + H** Active
11 Possessive pronouns	**H** Receptive
12 Indefinite pronouns	**F + H** Active

Verbs

The most important part of a sentence is the verb. It is a word which shows an action. Dictionaries list verbs by the present infinitive forms, such as manger = to eat.

There are three main groups of French verbs related to the last two letters of the present infinitive.

- Group 1 **er** (such as donn**er**)
- Group 2 **ir** (such as fin**ir**)
- Group 3 **re** (such as vend**re**)

Remove the last two letters of the infinitive to get the 'stem' of the verb.

Infinitive – regarder: regard = stem

You need the stems of the verbs in the three groups to form the different tenses (using time zones); these will help you talk about past, present and future events. You also need the stem of the verb so that you can add the appropriate ending for the subject of the verb or the person performing the action.

Remember, if you are using the person's name (Paul or Anne) use the part of the verb that goes with il or elle. For more than one person (Paul et Anne) use the part of the verb that goes with ils.

Irregular verbs, those that don't follow any of the patterns of the three main groups, are listed under each tense.

1 Present Tense

When is it used?

To talk about an action happening now or which happens normally: such as I eat at 6 o'clock or I am eating = je mange.

- Group 1 -**er** verbs, such as donner
  Add -e, -es, -e, -ons, -ez or -ent to the stem.
  For example:

je donn**e**	= I give / am giving
tu donn**es**	= you give / are giving
il / elle / on donn**e**	= he / she / one gives / is giving
nous donn**ons**	= we give / are giving
vous donn**ez**	= you give / are giving
ils / elles donn**ent**	= they give / are giving

- Group 2 -**ir** verbs, such as finir
  Add -is, -is, -it, -issons, -issez or -issent to the stem.

je fin**is**	= I finish / am finishing
tu fin**is**	
il / elle / on fin**it**	
nous fin**issons**	
vous fin**issez**	
ils / elles fin**issent**	

- Group 3 -**re** verbs, such as vendre
  Add s, -s, __, -ons, -ez or -ent to the stem.

je vend**s**	= I sell / am selling
tu vend**s**	
il / elle / on vend	
nous vend**ons**	
vous vend**ez**	
ils / elles vend**ent**	

Important irregular verbs. Look up the infinitive in a dictionary if you are unsure about the meaning.

APPELER = to call

j'appelle
tu appelles
il / elle / on appelle
nous appelons
vous appelez
ils / elles appellent

AVOIR = to have

j'ai
tu as
il / elle / on a
nous avons
vous avez
ils / elles ont

ETRE = to be

je suis
tu es
il / elle / on est
nous sommes
vous êtes
ils / elles sont

COURIR = to run

je cours
tu cours
il / elle / on court
nous courons
vous courez
ils / elles courent

DORMIR = to sleep

je dors
tu dors
il / elle / on dort
nous dormons
vous dormez
ils / elles dorment

FAIRE = to do, make

je fais
tu fais
il / elle / on fait
nous faisons
vous faites
ils / elles font

LIRE = to read

je lis
tu lis
il / elle lit
nous lisons
vous lisez
ils / elles lisent

METTRE = to put

je mets
tu mets
il / elle / on met
Nous mettons
vous mettez
ils / elles mettent

VENIR = to come

je viens
tu viens
il / elle on vient
nous venons
vous venez
ils / elles viennent

Reflexive verbs

A reflexive action is an action done to oneself.

se laver = to wash (oneself)
je me lave
tu te laves
il / elle / on se lave
nous nous lavons
vous vous lavez
ils / elles se lavent

Present tense + depuis

Je mange depuis une heure.	= I have been eating for an hour.
Je regarde la télévision depuis dix minutes.	= I have been watching television for ten minutes.

2 Perfect Tense

Going for a C?

You should be confident about using this tense; make the most of the mind maps on pages 101, 106 and 123.

When is it used?

To describe a **finished** action (in the past), e.g. I got up, I ate breakfast, I went to school.

All verbs need:

a a helper (auxiliary) verb.
This is part of avoir or être in the present, such as j'ai / je suis (see page 141).

b a past participle (see below).

Revise the verbs avoir and être (present tense).

Which auxiliary verb: Avoir or être?

Nearly all of them take avoir!
But here's an easy way to remember the verbs that are formed with être; use the mnemonic MR VANS TRAMPED!

M	monter	= to go up
R	rester	= to stay
V	venir (also revenir)	= to come (back)
A	aller	= to go
N	naître	= to be born
S	sortir	= to go out
T	tomber	= to fall
R	retourner	= to return
A	arriver	= to arrive
M	mourir	= to die
P	partir	= to leave
E	entrer (also rentrer)	= to go (back) in
D	descendre	= to go down

How does it work?

Choose the correct part of avoir or être to go with the subject, such as j'ai or je suis. Then you need the past participle.

How do I get the past participle?

- Group 1 verbs -er (donner)
  add é   to the stem   (donné*)
- Group 2 verbs -ir (finir)
  add i   to the stem   (fini)
- Group 3 verbs -re (vendre)
  add u   to the stem   (vendu)

*You should *never* forget this accent on the é – it's very important, without it, the meaning can change.

Now put the two together:

j'ai mangé = I ate
j'ai regardé = I watched

With avoir, past participles don't agree with the person performing the action (so don't add -e, -s or -es). Preceding direct object agreements – see Pronouns 2 (on pages 152–153). However, with être, past participles do agree.

How does the past participle agree?

Once you know which verbs take être, it gets easier! Remember MR VANS TRAMPED.

a use the correct form of être, such as je suis.

b form the past participle using the above rules:

find the stem	add the correct ending
aller – all:	allé (past participle)
sortir – sort:	sorti
descendre – descend:	descendu
Example: je suis allé = I went	

> **Watch out for these exceptions!**
> mourir: **mort**
> naître: **né**
> venir: **venu**

BEWARE you must make être past participles agree with the gender of the person performing the action …

FEMALE	MALE
je suis allé**e** (add an -e)	je suis allé (nothing added)
tu es allé**e**	tu es allé
elle est allé**e**	il est allé

… and with the number of people performing the action.

PLURAL FEMININE	PLURAL MASCULINE
nous sommes allé**es**	nous sommes allés
vous êtes allé**es**	vous êtes allés
elles sont allé**es**	ils sont allés

Remember:
MR VANS TRAMPED past participles agree!

Irregular verbs all use avoir as the auxiliary. Learn the past participles carefully!

avoir: j'ai eu	= I had
boire: j'ai bu	= I drank
conduire: j'ai conduit	= I drove
dire: j'ai dit	= I said
écrire: j'ai écrit	= I wrote
être: j'ai été	= I have been
faire: j'ai fait	= I did / I made
lire: j'ai lu	= I read
mettre: j'ai mis	= I put
ouvrir: j'ai ouvert	= I opened
prendre: j'ai pris	= I took
savoir: j'ai su	= I know
voir: j'ai vu	= I saw
voulour: j'ai voulu	= I wanted

Reflexive verbs use être as the auxiliary.

> je me suis levé(e) = I got up
> tu t'es levé(e)
> il s'est levé
> elle s'est levée
> nous nous sommes levé(e)s
> vous vous êtes levé(e)s
> ils se sont levés
> elles se sont levées

3 Imperfect Tense

Some exam boards require you to produce this tense in the Speaking and Writing skills as well as recognise it if you are Going for a C. The imperfect, also a past tense, describes **un**finished actions whereas the perfect tense describes finished actions.

Here's a summary of the main uses of the imperfect tense:

i to describe something which **used** to happen regularly or repeatedly.

| J'**allais** au cinéma tous les vendredis. | = I used to go to the cinema on Fridays. |

ii to describe something which was happening (imperfect) when something else happened (perfect).

| Je **regardais** la télévision quand ma mère est entrée dans la pièce. | = I was watching TV when my mother came into the room. |

iii to describe people, weather or things in the past.

Le château **était** beau.	= The castle was beautiful.
J'**étais** content(e) / triste.	= I was happy / sad.
Quand je me suis levé(e), il **faisait** soleil.	= When I got up, it was sunny.

Here's a clue! If the English = 'was + ing', such as I was watching TV, use the imperfect tense of the verb which has 'ing'.

| Je regardais. | = I was watching. |

How do I form the imperfect?

a take the nous form of the present tense. Then remove the -ons.

> donner – nous donnons: donn
> finir – nous finissons: finiss
> vendre – nous vendons: vend

b add the following endings -ais, -ais, -ait, -ions, -iez, or -aient.

je donnais	nous donnions
tu donnais	vous donniez
il / elle / on donnait	ils / elles donnaient

Note this important irregular verb: être

| j'étais | tu étais | il était |
| nous étions | vous étiez | ils étaient |

il y avait = there was / there were
Il y avait beaucoup de monde. = There were a lot of people.

C'était chouette! = It was great!

C'était fermé. = It was closed.

4 Future Tense

Going for a C or an A?

You should be able to talk and write about events in the future.

How do I form the future?

- Group 1 ER and Group 2 IR verbs
    a take the infinitive, such as donner, finir.
    b add -ai, -as, -a, -ons, -ez or -ont:
    > je donnerai = I will give
    > tu donneras
    > il / elle / on donnera
    > nous donnerons
    > vous donnerez
    > ils donneront
- Group 3 RE verbs
    a remove the -e from the infinitive, then add the endings as above.

Watch out for irregular verbs!

They have unusual stems, but the endings are as above.

acheter: j'achèterai	mourir: je mourrai
= I will buy	pleuvoir: il pleuvra
aller : j'irai = I will go	= it will rain
appeler: j'appellerai	pouvoir: je pourrai
avoir: j'aurai	recevoir: je recevrai
courir: je courrai	savoir: je saurai
devoir: je devrai	venir: je viendrai
envoyer: j'enverrai	voir: je verrai
être: je serai	vouloir: je voudrai
faire: je ferai	

In English you often use the present tense where the French use the future.

Elle arrivera (future) quand elle sera (future) prête.	= She will arrive (future) when she is (present) ready.

Use the future after quand in such cases.

How can I avoid the 'future'?

Use the 'near future'! This is easy to use and is like the English – I am going to do something. Use the correct form of aller + an infinitive.

Je vais manger.	= I am going to eat.
Tu vas sortir.	= You are going to go out.
Il / elle / on va danser.	= He / she / one is going to dance.
Nous allons partir.	= We are going to leave.
Vous allez chanter.	= You are going to sing.
Ils / elles vont aller au café.	= They are going to go to the café.

5 Pluperfect Tense

Some exam boards do not require the active use of this tense, but others do if you are aiming for an A or B grade. If you are Going for a C you should at least recognise it. This tense describes what *had* happened before something else happened (perfect).

How do I form the pluperfect?

Use the imperfect tense of:
either
avoir + past participle.

J'avais mangé.	= I had eaten.

or
être + past participle.

J'étais partie(e).	= I had left.

Here's a helpful clue! Verbs which take être in the perfect (MR VANS TRAMPED) also take être in the pluperfect, and the past participle agrees.

ALLER	DONNER
j'étais allé(e) = I had gone	j'avoir donné = I had given
tu étais allé(e)	tu avais donné
il était allé	il avait donné
elle était allée	elle avait donné
nous étions allé(e)s	nous avions donné
vous étiez allé(e)s	vous aviez donné
ils étaient allés	ils avaient donné
elles étaient allées	elles avaient donné

Reflexive verbs take être (as in the perfect).

Je m'étais levé(e).	= I had got up.

6 Past Historic Tense

This tense is used in newspaper articles and novels. It is used to write about events in the past (like the perfect), but you won't have to produce it yourself. You might come across it in a reading exercise, so you must be able to recognise it.

Here are the endings.
- Group 1 ER verbs:
  -ai, -as, -a, -âmes, -âtes, -èrent
  For example: je donnai = I gave
- Group 2 IR verbs + Group 3 RE verbs:
  -is, -is, -it, -îmes, -îtes, -irent
  For example: je finis = I finished, je descendis = I went down

Irregular verbs with unusual stems!

je conduisis = I drove	je pris = I took
je dis = I said	je ris = I laughed
j'écrivis = I wrote	je vins = I came
je fis = I made	je vis = I saw
je mis = I put	

7 Conditional Tense

This tense describes what **would** happen. You are already familiar with: je voudrais = I would like.

It is often used with an imperfect tense, and si (if).

Si j'avais beaucoup d'argent, j'**irais** en France.	= If I had a lot of money, I **would go** to France.

How do I form the conditional?

a Group 1 + 2 verbs take the infinitive, and Group 3 verbs remove the e from the infinitive.
ER verbs, e.g. donner
IR verbs, e.g. finir
RE verbs, e.g. vendr
b add -ais, -ais, -ait, -ions, -iez or -aient:
Je donnerais. = I would give.

Irregular verbs:
Look back at the unusual stems used in the future (on page 143); these are the same for the conditional with the above endings.

ACHETER (infinitive)
j'**achèterai** (future)
j'**achèterais** (conditional)

ALLER (infinitive)
j'**ir**ai (future)
j'**ir**ais (conditional)

Watch out for these!

j'aurais = I would have
je serais = I would be
je ferais = I would do / make
je voudrais = I would like

8 Conditional Perfect Tense

 Receptive

This translates as 'would have' or 'should have' done something. You only have to be able to recognise this in the exam, but if you can use it you will score 'bonus' marks!

How is it formed?

a select an auxiliary verb (avoir or être) as you would for the perfect tense.
b put the auxiliary verb in the conditional.

AVOIR	ETRE
j'aurais = I would have	je serais = I would like
tu aurais	tu serais
il aurait	il serait
nous aurions	nous serions
vous auriez	vous seriez
ils auraient	ils seraient

c add the past participle. Remember agreements on past participles using être.

MANGER	ALLER
j'aurais mangé = I would have eaten	je serais allé(e) = I would have gone
tu aurais mangé	tu serais allé(e)
il / elle / on aurait mangé	il / on serait allé / elle serait allée
vous auriez mangé	vous seriez allé(e)(s)
ils auraient mangé	ils seraient allés
elles auraient mangé	elles seraient allées

9 Venir de + Infinitive

 Active

Use the *present* tense of venir + an infinitive.

Je viens de manger.	= I have just eaten.
Je viens de partir.	= I have just left.
Tu viens de finir.	= You have just finished.

Il / elle vient de sortir.	= He / she has just gone out.
Nous venons de manger.	= We have just eaten.
Vous venez d'arriver.	= You have just arrived.
Ils viennent de finir.	= They have just finished.

This construction can also be used with the imperfect tense of venir + an infinitive:

Je venais (imperfect) de manger.	= I *had* just eaten.
Elle venait de partir.	= She had just left.

10 Present Subjunctive

 Receptive

Going for an A?

Then you just need to be able to recognise this form which is usually close to the present tense.

Il faut que je mange.	= It is necessary that I (should) eat.

Watch out for these irregular forms!

aller: j'aille	faire: je fasse
avoir: j'aie	pouvoir: je puisse
boire: je boive	savoir: je sache
être: je sois	

11 Present Participle

 Receptive / Active

This translates as the 'ing' form of English verbs.

allant = going
donnant = giving

BEWARE! Don't use this where all you need is the present tense.

Je vais.	= I am going.

A present participle is not complete in itself and is best used alongside another verb (see examples below).

How do I form it?

a take the nous form of the present tense such as allons, donnons, finissons, vendons.
b remove the -ons ending.
c add -ant:
allant = going
donnant = giving
finissant = finishing
vendant = selling

Watch out for these irregular present participles!

avoir: ayant   savoir: sachant   être: étant

Étant riche, elle a acheté beaucoup de cadeaux.	= Being rich, she bought lots of presents.
Voyant qu'il était en retard, il s'est dépêché.	= Seeing that he was late, he hurried up.

The present participle is often used with en = by / while / on doing.

En travaillant dur, elle a réussi à ses examens.	= By working hard she passed her exams.
Il a écouté ses CD en faisant ses devoirs.	= He listened to his CDs while doing his homework.
Elle est rentrée en courant.	= She went running home.

12 Infinitives

Some verbs can be followed by another as in English.

J'aime jouer au tennis.	= I like to play (playing) tennis.
Je veux sortir.	= I want to go out.
Je sais nager.	= I know how to swim.

The basic rule is, as in English, if there are two verbs together, the second is the infinitive form.

J'adore aller au cinéma.	= I love going to the cinema.
J'espère y aller.	= I hope to go there.
Il préfère manger du poisson.	= He prefers to eat fish.
Elle déteste écrire des lettres.	= She hates writing letters.

- Some verbs are always followed with **à** before the infinitive; try to learn the following common ones:
  aider à: J'aide à faire la vaisselle. = I help to wash up.

commencer à	inviter à
continuer à	se mettre à
se décider à	passer du temps à
demander à	réussir à
hésiter à	

- Other verbs are always followed with **de** before an infinitive; try these:
  décider de: J'ai décidé de sortir. = I decided to go out.

s'arrêter de	offrir de
cesser de	oublier de
décider de	permettre de
dire de	refuser de
essayer de	regretter de
finir de	

avoir besoin de	avoir peur de
avoir le droit de	avoir l'intention de

- sans + infinitive = without

Je suis partie **sans dire** 'au revoir'.	= I left **without saying** goodbye.

- pour + infinitive = in order to

Je travaille **pour réussir** à mes examens!	= I am working in order to pass my exams.

Remember don't use pour after attendre, chercher or payer.

J'attends le bus.	= I'm waiting for the bus.
Je cherche mon stylo.	= I'm looking for my pen.

13 Perfect Infinitive

This is the equivalent of 'after having done' something.

Après avoir mangé, je suis parti(e).	= After having eaten, I left.

Notice the subject of the two verbs is the same.

Après avoir regardé la télévision, j'ai fait mes devoirs.	= After having watched (watching) TV, I did my homework.

How do I form it?

a   use après + être (if verbs take être in the perfect),
     or après + avoir (if verbs take avoir in the perfect).
b   add the past participle.
c   if using an être verb make the past participle agree with the subject (remember: MR VANS TRAMPED verb).

If it's a woman talking:

Après être arrivée, j'ai pris le dîner.	= After I had arrived, I had dinner.

14 Negatives

In French, the negative form of a verb has two parts such as ne ... pas.

The **ne** goes in front of the verb and the **pas** goes after the verb.

Je ne regarde pas le télévision. = I don't watch TV.
Je n'aime pas les maths. = I don't like maths.
Je ne me lève pas tôt. = I don't get up early.

In the perfect tense the ne and pas go either side of the auxiliary verb (avoir or être).

Je n'ai pas mangé. = I didn't eat.
Je ne suis pas sorti(e). = I didn't go out.

After a negative and to translate 'any' use de or d' before a noun.

Je n'ai pas d'argent. = I haven't got any money.

Other useful negatives

ne ... rien = nothing
ne ... jamais = never
ne ... plus = no longer

Je ne comprends rien. = I understand nothing
(I don't understand anything).

Here are some more useful negatives. These operate so that the second part (such as aucun, que) goes *after* the past participle.

ne ... aucun = no, not a
ne ... que = only
ne ... personne = nobody
ne ... ni ... ni = neither ... nor

Il n'a eu aucun problème. = He had no problem.
Elle n'a payé que 10 francs. = She only paid 10 francs.
Je n'ai vu personne. = I saw nobody.
Il n'a mangé ni les bananes, = He ate neither the
ni les pommes. bananas nor the apples.

15 Imperatives

This is used to tell somebody what to do, as a request or an order. There are three forms:

i The 'vous' form; used to one person you do not know well, or two or more people.

ii The 'tu' form; used to one person you know well.

iii The 'nous' form; used to mean 'let's do something'.

How do I form the imperative?

a use the 'vous' form of the present tense and drop the vous.
Regardez! Ecoutez! = Look! Listen!

b use the 'tu' form of the present tense and drop the tu.
Finis ton travail! = Finish your work!

Note that with an ER verb, you must drop the final -s.
Regarde! Ecoute! = Look! Listen!

c use the 'nous' form of the present tense and drop the nous.
Partons! = Let's go!

What about the imperative with reflexive verbs?

You'll need a reflexive pronoun.

Levez-vous! Lève-toi! = Get up!

Note that **te** becomes **toi** in the imperative.

Watch out for these exceptions!

AVOIR	ETRE
(i) ayez = have	(i) soyez = be
(ii) aie = have	(ii) sois = be
(iii) ayons = let's have	(iii) soyons = let's be

16 Interrogatives

There are three ways to ask questions.

* Inversion (turning the subject and verb round) and add a hyphen.
Tu manges: Manges-tu?
Tu as mangé: As-tu mangé?
Il est parti: Est-il parti?
Elle a mangé: A-t*-elle mangé? (* Put in the t between the vowels)

* A more formal way of asking a question. Use intonation (raising your voice at the end of the sentence).
Tu as fini. = You have finished.
Tu as fini? = Have you finished?

* Place Est-ce que / qu'? before a statement.
Il aime le foot. (statement) = He likes football.
Est-ce qu'il aime le foot? = Does he like
(question) football?

Common question words (see Pronouns 9 on page 154).

Combien ... de ...? = How much /
How many ...?

Comment ...? = How / What?
D'où ...? = From where?
Où ...? = Where?
Pourquoi ...? = Why?
Quand ...? = When?
Qui ...? = Who?

Here are two more forms that must agree with the noun following.

Quel / Quelle / Quels / Quelles?	= Which?
Que / Qu' ...?	= What?

17 Passive Voice Receptive

This is used when the person or thing performing the action (the subject) is also at the receiving end of the action,

J'ai été mordu par le chien.	= I've been bitten by the dog.
Il a été blessé.	= He's been injured.

But note this example where the past participle agrees with the subject.

Elle a été blessée.	= She's been injured.

How can I avoid the passive?

- Use 'on'.
  On a trouvé le chien. = The dog was found.
- Use an active verb.
  Un moustique l'a piquée. = A mosquito stung her.
- Use an impersonal verb.
  Il est interdit de stationner. = No parking.

Nouns

1 Gender Active

All nouns are either masculine or feminine (m. or f. in dictionaries). People's names usually take the gender you'd expect such as le père (m.), la mère (f.).

Some nouns are always masculine, whether the person is male or female, such as le médecin, le professeur (although you may hear la prof in conversation).

Typical masculine endings: -ier, -eau, -ment and -age.

Watch out for these exceptions!		
la page	la plage	l'eau
la cage	une image	la peau

Typical feminine endings: -ade, -ance, -ence, -ière, -ille, -ine, -ion, -té and -tié.

Watch out for these exceptions!		
le silence	le camion	un été
le million	le côté	

There are some nouns that have both a masculine and a feminine form, such as un acteur / une actrice, un ami / une amie.

BEWARE some words have two meanings. Here are some of the most common.

le livre = the book	la livre = £ (sterling)
le manche = the handle	la Manche = the Channel
	la manche = the sleeve
le voile = the veil	la voile = the sail

2 Definite Article (the + noun) Active

Singular		Plural		
Masculine	Feminine	Masculine	Feminine	
le / l'	la / l'	les	les	= the
au / à l'	à la / à l'	aux	aux	= to the
du / de l'	de la / de l'	des	des	= of the

Note that French uses a definite article where there wouldn't be one in English.

- parts of the body.
  Elle a *les* yeux verts. = She has green eyes.
  Il s'est cassé *la* jambe. = He broke his leg.
- for nouns used in a general way.
  J'adore *le* fromage. = I love cheese.
- for languages, countries.
  J'aime *la* France. = I like France.
  J'aime étudier *le* français. = I like studying French(!).

3 Indefinite Article (a, some) Active

Singular		Plural		
Masc.	Fem.	Masc.	Fem.	
un	une	= a, an des	des	= some, any

Remember that des becomes de if an adjective is used before a plural noun. For example: de grandes maisons.

Note these rules:

- use de / d' in a negative construction.
  Je n'ai pas d'argent.   = I haven't any money.
- use the indefinite article in lists.
  J'ai acheté des fleurs, des   = I've bought flowers,
  chocolats et des souvenirs.   chocolates and souvenirs.

BUT do **not** use an indefinite article for jobs.

Mon père est médecin.   = My father is a doctor.

4 Partitive Article (some, any)

Singular		Plural		
Masculine	Feminine	Masculine	Feminine	
du / de l'	de la / de l'	des	des	= some, any

- Use de l' in front of a masculine or feminine singular noun beginning with a vowel or an 'h', such as l'eau, l'hôtel.

du vin   = some wine
de la viande   = some meat
des fleurs   = some flowers

beaucoup de vin,   = lots of wine,
assez de fruits,   = enough fruits
trop de bruit   = too much noise

5 Plurals

Don't forget to change the article and the noun for the plural forms.
le garçon: les garçons   une fille: des filles
un garçon: des garçons   la fille: les filles

Many nouns add -s to become plural (as above) but others change their ending.
-al: **-aux**   un cheval: des chevaux
au / **-eu**: **-x**   un oiseau: des oiseaux

-s, -x, or -z don't change in the plural.
le nez: les nez
le bras: les bras

Nouns ending in -ou add -s.
un trou: les trous

6 Possession

Remember that in French there's never an apostrophe to show that something belongs to somebody. Use de + name.

Le vélo de Paul.   = Paul's bike.

Adjectives

1 Forming Adjectives

Adjectives change their spellings so that they agree with the noun in number (singular / plural) and gender (masculine / feminine).

How does an adjective agree?

	Singular			Plural
Masculine	Action needed!		Feminine	Masculine / Feminine
petit	Add -e for feminine and -s for plural.		petit**e**	petit**s** / petit**es**
jeune	*Adjective ends in -e* Add -s for plural but no -e for feminine.		jeune	jeune**s** / jeune**s**
gris	*Adjective ends in -s* Add -e for feminine but no extras.		gris**e**	gris / gris**e**
premier	*Adjective ends in -ier* Add acute accent and -e in feminine singular, and -s in plural.		premi**ère**	premier**s** / premi**ères**
heureux	*Adjective ends in -eux* Change -x to -s in feminine.		heureu**se**	heureux / heureu**ses**
actif	*Adjective ends in -f* Change -f to -v in feminine before adding endings.		acti**ve**	actif**s** / acti**ves**

Note that the following compound (two used together) adjectives do not agree with the noun:

une jupe bleu clair   = a light blue skirt
une robe blue marine   = a navy blue dress
des baskets jaune pâle   = some light yellow trainers
des baskets vert foncé   = some dark green trainers

Common irregular adjectives to learn!

Singular		Plural	
Masculine	Feminine	Masculine	Feminine
ancien	ancienne	anciens	anciennes
beau (bel*)	belle	beaux	belles
blanc	blanche	blancs	blanches
bon	bonne	bons	bonnes
cher	chère	chers	chères
favori	favorite	favoris	favorites
faux	fausse	faux	fausses
frais	fraîche	frais	fraîches
gentil	gentille	gentils	gentilles
long	longue	longs	longues
neuf	neuve	neufs	neuves
nouveau (nouvel*)	nouvelle	nouveaux	nouvelles
public	publique	publics	publiques
secret	secrète	secrets	secrètes
vieux (vieil*)	vieille	vieux	vieilles

* These forms are used before masculine singular words beginning with a vowel or silent h: such as un vieil homme.

Where do I place the adjective?

Place these adjectives before the noun:

beau	grand	joli	petit
bon	gros	long	vieux
court	haut	mauvais	
gentil	jeune	meilleur	

Place other adjectives after the noun.

| une vieille voiture française | = an old French car |
| le petit train jaune | = the little yellow train |

Remember some adjectives can go before or after the noun and can change their meaning depending on their position. See propre (below).

ancien = former / old
| mon ancien collège | = my former (ex) school |
| un collège ancien | = an old school |

cher = dear / expensive
| mon cher cousin | = my dear cousin |
| un pullover cher | = an expensive pullover |

dernier = latest / last
| le dernier CD de Céline Dion | = Céline Dion's latest CD |
| la semaine dernière | = last week |

grand = great / tall
| un grand homme | = a great man |
| un homme grand | = a tall man |

propre = own / clean
| Elle a sa propre voiture. | = She's got her own car. |
| La voiture propre. | = The clean car. |

2 Possessive Adjectives

These go in front of nouns to show who owns what!

Remember that the form you use depends not on the gender of the owner (the 'his' or 'hers') but on the gender of the thing they own (in these examples the brother and the car).

son frère (frère is masculine)	= his brother
son frère (frère is masculine)	= her brother
sa voiture (voiture is feminine)	= his car
sa voiture (voiture is feminine)	= her car

Singular		Plural	
Masculine	Feminine	Masculine / Feminine	
mon	ma (mon*)	mes	= my
ton	ta (ton*)	tes	= your
son	sa (son*)	ses	= his / her
notre	notre	nos	= our
votre	votre	vos	= your
leur	leur	leurs	= their

*Use before a singular feminine noun which begins with a vowel or silent h, such as son amie.

3 Demonstrative Adjectives

These are used before nouns and mean:
singular – this, that   plural – these, those

Singular		Plural
Masculine	Feminine	Masculine / Feminine
ce, cet	cette	ces

cette femme	= this / that woman
ce stylo	= this / that pen
ces enfants	= these / those children

For emphasis you can add ci or là.

| ce stylo-ci / là | = this pen (here / there) |

4 Comparatives
(how to say something is more than something else)

• use plus before the French adjective to say 'more' or the 'er' form of the English adjective.
| J'ai une plus grande chambre. | = I've got a bigger bedroom. |

Comparing two things

aussi ... que = as ... as,   moins ... que = less ... than plus ... que = more than

Il est *plus* grand *que* sa soeur.	= He is taller / bigger than his sister.
Il est *moins* intelligent *que* sa soeur.	= He is less intelligent than his sister.
Elle est *aussi* gentille *que* son frère.	= She is as nice as her brother.
Note: Elle n'est pas *si* gentille.	= She is not as nice.

You should use si after a negative.

Note: use meilleur(e)(s) for better.

Comparing more than two things: superlatives

These are adjectives such as *the* best and *the* worst.

le plus / moins + masculine singular adjective
la plus / moins + feminine singular adjective
les plus / moins + masc. / fem. plural adjectives

Le train le plus rapide.	= The fastest train.
La chanson la plus célèbre.	= The most famous song.
bon = good	
le / la meilleur(e)	= the best
mauvais = bad	
le / la pire	
le / la plus mauvais(e)	= the worst
petit = small	
le / la plus petit(e)	= the smallest
le / la moindre	= the slightest

5 Indefinite Adjectives

autre(s) = other	
les autres garçons	= the other boys
chaque = each	
chaque élève	= each pupil
même(s) = same	
la même trousse	= the same pencil case
les mêmes livres	= the same books
tout / toute / tous / toutes + article = all	
tout le vin	= all the wine
toute la famille	= all the family
tous les livres	= all the books
toutes les fleurs	= all the flowers
plusieurs = several	
plusieurs livres	= several books
quelque(s) = some	
quelques garçons	= some boys (several)
tel / telle / tels / telles = such	
un tel homme	= such a man
une telle histoire	= such a story

Adverbs

Adverbs give us more information about verbs, such as well, slowly: She sings (verb) *well* (adverb); he walks (verb) *slowly* (adverb).

1 Formation

Simply use the feminine form of the adjective and add -ment.

heureuse: heureusement = happily

Watch out for these exceptions!

constamment = constanty	gentiment = nicely
énormément = enormously	mal = badly
évidemment = evidently	poliment = politely
précisément = precisely	
vraiment* = truly / really	

* If the masculine form of the adjective ends in i or u add -ment.

Normally, you put the adverb after the verb, but in the perfect tense the adverb nearly always goes between the auxiliary and the past participle.

Il a souvent parlé.	= He often talked.
Elle a trop mangé.	= She ate too much.

Adverbs of time go after the past participle. Examples of these are: tard = late, hier = yesterday.

Je suis arrivé hier.	= I arrived yesterday.

Watch out for these adverbs!

avec soin = carefully	tard = late
beaucoup = a lot	tôt = early
longtemps = for a long time	trop = too much
mal = badly	vite = quickly
mieux = better	

2 Comparatives and Superlatives

As with adjectives, use: plus = more, moins = less, aussi ... = as.

Il a marché aussi lentement que sa soeur.	= He walked as slowly as his sister.

Plus, moins or aussi go before the adverb whereas que follows the adverb.

12

The superlative of adverbs is formed by using le plus or le moins + the adverb. No agreements are necessary here as the superlative describes the *action* of the person not the person. Le plus therefore does not change to la plus or les plus.

Il conduit le plus vite.	= He drives the fastest.
Elle conduit le plus vite.	= She drives the fastest.

Remember that the adverb **bien** (= well) becomes **mieux** (= better) and **le mieux** (= best).

Elle travaille le mieux.	= She works the best.

Pronouns

(words which stand in place of nouns)

1 Subject Pronouns

A subject pronoun tells you who or what is performing an action. Remember ils (they, is used for a mixed group, ie masculine + feminine nouns together.

Les garçons + les filles = ils

Ils vont au café.	= They are going to the café.

2 Direct Object Pronouns

A direct object is the person or the thing at the receiving end of the verb:

Il   me   regarde. = He is watching me.
↓   ↓   ↓
subject   object   verb

Je mange la pomme.	= I eat **the apple**.
Je **la** mange.	= I eat it (la replaces la pomme).
Je ne la mange pas.	= I don't eat it.

The direct object pronoun goes before the verb and after the subject.

Preceding direct object + agreement

In the perfect tense, the direct object pronoun goes before the past participle and makes it agree. Add the agreements according to the gender of the direct object, not the gender of the subject.

J'ai mangé **la pomme**: Je l'ai mang**ée** (add **-e**).
J'ai acheté les pommes: Je **les** ai achet**ées** (add **-es**).
J'ai vu **le** garçon: Je l'ai vu (no agreement).
J'ai vu les garçons: Je les ai vu**s** (add -s).

3 Indirect Object Pronouns

These pronouns replace à + noun (to the boy – to him – lui). They are used with verbs which are followed by à:

demander à	répondre à
dire à	ressembler à
offrir à	téléphoner à
parler à	

Il **m**'a demandé.	= He asked **me**. (to me)
Elle **lui** a dit que.	= She told **him / her** that . (to him / her)
Je **leur** ai offert un cadeau.	= I gave **them** a present. (to them)
Ils **lui** ont parlé.	= They spoke to **him / her**. (to him / her)
Elle m'a téléphoné.	= She phoned **me**. (to me)

1 Subject Pronouns		**2** Direct Object Pronouns		**3** Indirect Object Pronouns	
je	I	me (m')	me	me (m')	of, to, for me
tu	you	te (t')	you	te (t')	of, to, for you
il	he	le (l')	him	lui	of, to, for himself
elle	she	la (l')	her	lui	of, to, for herself
on	one	se (s')	himself / herself / oneself	se (s')	of, to, for himself / herself / oneself
nous	we	nous	us	nous	of, to, for us
vous	you	vous	you	vous	of, to, for you
ils	they	les	them	leur	of, to, for them
elles	they	les	them	leur	of, to, for them

4 En

This pronoun replaces a word which begins with du / de la / de l' / des (of it, of them, some, any, from it, from them). It goes before the verb.

Tu as **des stylos?**
Oui, j'**en** ai deux.   = I've got two **of them.**
Tu veux **du fromage**?
Oui j'**en** veux.   = I'd like **some.**

5 Y

Y means 'there' when referring to a place already mentioned. It replaces à + place.

Je vais **au café**.
J'**y** vais.   = I go **there.**

6 Position of Pronouns

Generally, pronouns go before the verb, and in compound tenses (tenses such as the perfect, pluperfect) they go before the auxiliary verb. The exception to this rule is when you tell somebody what to do and use an imperative.

Regarde-la!   = Look at her.
Donnez-moi le stylo!   = Give me the pen.

Note that me and te become moi and toi in the Imperative. If you tell somebody **not** to do something then the pronoun goes in front of the verb and is in its usual form.

Ne **la** regarde pas!   = Don't look at her.
Ne **me** donnez pas le stylo!   = Don't give me the pen.

Order of Object Pronouns
If you use two or more, do so in this order:

me				
te	le			
se	la	lui	y	en
nous	les	leur		
vous				

Je la lui donne.   = I give it to her.

7 Emphatic Pronouns
(stressed or disjunctive pronouns)

If you want to use a pronoun by itself such as it's **me**, some pronouns have special forms:

moi = me	nous = us
toi = you	vous = you
lui = him	eux = them
elle = her	elles = them

Use these:
* after prepositions: avec **moi** = with me
* if the pronoun stands by itself
  Qui l'a fait? **Moi!**   = Who did it? Me!
* with même
  Je l'ai fait moi-même.   = I did it myself.
* to emphasise subject pronouns
  Moi, je ne veux pas sortir.   = I don't want to go out!

8 Relative Pronouns

* Qui = who: used as the subject of a clause which follows:
  Le livre **qui** est sur la table.   = The book **which** is on the table.

  ____ + verb: use qui.
  La femme **qui** habite en face.   = The lady **who** lives opposite.
* Que = whom / who: used as the object of a clause which follows.
  Les matières **que** je préfère.   = The subjects which I prefer.

  ____ + subject + verb → use que
* Dont = of which, of whom, whose
  Le disque **dont** je te parlais.   = The record I was telling you about.

  La fille **dont** le père est professeur.   = The girl whose father is a teacher.

* Lequel (m), laquelle (f), lesquels (mpl), lesquelles (fpl) = which use these pronouns after prepositions such as avec and dans when you are referring to things, not people. (For people use à qui.)

Remember to choose the pronoun according to the gender of the thing to which you are referring.

Le stylo avec lequel j'écris.   = The pen with which I write.

Note: If you link these words to à the form changes to: auquel, à laquelle, auxquels, auxquelles.

If you link these words to de the form changes to:
duquel   de laquelle   desquels   desquelles

9 Interrogative Pronouns

- Qui (subject) = Who? (talking about a person)

| Qui va en ville? / Qui est-ce qui va en ville? | = Who is going into town? |

- Qui (object) = who(m)?

| Qui est-ce que tu regardes? | = Who(m) are you watching. |

- Que (subject) = What? (talking about a thing)

| Qu'est-ce qui te surprend? | = What surprises you? |

- Que (object)

| Que fais-tu? / Qu'est-ce que tu fais? | = What are you doing? |

- (De)quoi = what?

| De quoi parles-tu? | = What are talking about? |

- Lequel / laquelle / lesquels / lesquelles = Which one(s)

| Laquelle des jupes est-ce que tu préfères? | = Which one of the skirts do you prefer? |

10 Demonstrative Pronouns

- ça / ce = this / that

| Regarde ça! | = Look at that. |

Note that ça is the shortened form of *cela*.

Note the use of cela.

| Avez-vous vu *cela* (or ça)? | = Have you seen that? |

Going for an A?

- celui (m/sing), celle (f/sing) = this one, that one, the one which

Quel livre?	
Celui qui est sur la table.	= The one which is on the table.
Celui-ci.	= This one here.
Quelle trousse?	
Celle qui est sur la table.	= The one which is on the table.
Celle-là.	= That one there.

- ceux (mpl), celles (fpl) = those ones

Quels livres?	
Ceux qui sont sur la table.	= The ones which are on the table.
Ceux-là.	= Those ones there.

Quelles trousses?	
Celles qui sont sur la table.	= The ones which are on the table.
Celles-ci.	= These ones here.

11 Possessive Pronouns

	M Sing	Fem Sing	M Plural	Fem Plural
mine	le mien	la mienne	les miens	les miennes
yours	le tien	la tienne	les tiens	les tiennes
his	le sien	la sienne	les siens	les siennes
hers	le sien	la sienne	les siens	les siennes
ours	le nôtre	la nôtre	les nôtres	les nôtres
yours	le vôtre	la vôtre	les vôtres	les vôtres
theirs	le leur	la leur	les leurs	les leurs

The choice of form depends on the gender of the noun, not on the gender of the owner,

| C'est la trousse de Paul. | |
| C'est la sienne. | = It's his. |

12 Indefinite Pronouns

- **quelqu'un** = somebody

| Il y a quelqu'un dans la maison. | = There is somebody in the house. |

- autre, chacun, plusieurs, quelques-uns / quelques-unes, tout:

  autre = other(s)

| Où sont les autres? | = Where are the others. |

  chacun / chacune = each (one).

| Chacun des garçons, chacune des filles, chacun va payer. | = Each one is going to pay. |

  n'importe qui = anybody

| N'importe qui peut le faire. | = Anybody can do it. |

  plusieurs = several.

| Tu as des CD? Oui, j'en ai plusieurs. | = I have several. |

  quelques-uns / quelques-unes = some (a few).

| Quelques-uns des garçons sont gentils. | = Some of the boys are nice. |
| Quelques-unes de ces assiettes sont sales. | = Some of these plates are dirty. |

  tout = everything.

| Je veux tout faire. | = I want to do everything. |
| Tout le monde est arrivé. | = Everybody has arrived. |

Index